YOUR UNTAMED TRUTHS

Reclaiming Self-Sovereignty

CAROLYN BROUILLARD

UNTAMED
PRESS

Your Untamed Truths: Reclaiming Self-Sovereignty

Copyright © 2026 by Carolyn Brouillard

All rights reserved. No part of this book may be reproduced, distributed, or transmitted in any form or by any means, including photocopying, recording, or other electronic or mechanical methods, without the prior written permission of the publisher, except in the case of brief quotations embodied in critical reviews and certain other noncommercial uses permitted by copyright law.

Privacy Note: This book includes personal stories to illustrate the concepts. The events are factual and drawn from my journals, correspondence, and memory. In honoring others' privacy, I have used pseudonyms and obscured certain identifying details.

Disclaimer: The insights shared in these pages are for educational and self-reflective purposes only. I am not a licensed medical, psychological, legal, or financial professional. Please consult qualified professionals for specific needs. The author and publisher disclaim liability arising from the use of information in this book.

Published by Untamed Press
www.untamedpress.com

ISBN: 979-8-9944336-0-7 (paperback)
ISBN: 979-8-9944336-1-4 (hardcover)
ISBN: 979-8-9944336-2-1 (ebook)

First Edition

Cover design by Anze Ban Virant - ABV Atelier Design
Interior design and formatting by Carolyn Brouillard
Author photo by Isabel Lawrence Photographers

This book is dedicated, with deep reverence, to all my teachers. You were my mirrors, my catalysts, and sometimes my "mistakes." But most of all, you were my fellow explorers on this magnificent human journey.

Contents

Preface	VII
Introduction	IX

Part I: Recognizing the Untamed Truths of You

1.	How Good Can It Get?	3
2.	What Matters Most	16
3.	Sketching Your Blueprint	26
4.	What You Came to Master	45
5.	Naming Your Life Intention	58
6.	How You Want to Live	68
7.	Architecting Your Life Design	76

Part II: Seeing Your Interference Patterns

8.	Understanding Coherence and Interference	85
9.	Running in the Shadows	98
10.	Static in Your Signal	117

Part III: Practicing Coherence and Self-Sovereignty

11.	The Two Questions That Change Everything	135

12.	When There Are Complications and Constraints	144
13.	The Relationship Realignment	156
14.	In The Chrysalis	168
15.	Emergence	178

Appendix

16.	Supplemental Exercises	187
17.	Coherence Audit: Weekly Reality Check	201

Acknowledgements	205
About the Author	207

Preface

I had a moment of déjà vu as I strolled through the venue for my book launch party. It wasn't a feeling that I had been there before—I knew I hadn't—but something about it felt familiar. That night, it hit me. Seven years ago, when the cracks started to appear in my corporate career, I wrote down a vision of my future.

One of my favorite scenes was standing in a room of smiling faces—book in hand—celebrating a dream come true. Touring the event space brought me back to that vision, now coming to fruition. Publishing a book that could change people's lives was part of it, but the larger vision was creating a beautiful and satisfying life, where I am free to follow my inspiration and imagination.

To those of you hungry for change, seven years might sound like a long time. But it feels fast when I compare my life then to my life now. I wasn't sitting around waiting for good things to happen—I was creating, course-correcting, and exploring. I had fun getting to know myself more deeply, becoming clearer on what I actually wanted, and trusting myself to experiment and play. I've been fine-tuning this life for the last seven years—and enjoying it along the way.

Coming into coherence—completely aligning my external self with my inner truth—was the final catalyst. It is what unlocked my vision and opened my eyes to new possibilities. This book distills a lifetime of seeking and learning into a practical framework that clarifies what matters most and what will fulfill you. It teaches coherence and the two questions that keep your signal strong. It worked for me, and I know it can work for you.

But first, you need to decide you are worthy of your own joy. You have to love yourself enough and care enough about your life to be willing to give yourself what you really want. You must be open to knowing yourself fully and meet that clarity with compassion and self-trust, while being unflinchingly honest about what's still holding you back. Unwavering authenticity isn't just about pursuing what lights you up—it's also about exposing where you still step into the shadows.

This doesn't mean digging in the dark. You don't need to know where a wound came from to heal it. You just need to see it and not let it choose for you. That is self-sovereignty: when fear is no longer the master, and your choices give you more of what you enjoy and less of what you don't. When you reclaim your sovereignty, you stop working against yourself—freeing yourself to honor the callings of your heart, the whispers of your intuition, and the wild visions of your imagination.

Every choice is a crossroads.

The question isn't whether you are worthy—you are.
The question is: *What is your life worth to you?*

My greatest hope is that you are willing to find out.

Introduction

When I was 18, I headed west with only a backpack and a dream of being free. For nearly two years, I rode freight trains through forests and deserts, hitchhiked along country roads and crowded highways, slept under bridges and beneath the stars. I lived hand-to-mouth and moment-to-moment with a tribe of outcasts doing the same. All of us running from something, toward something—caught between hope and despair.

It took courage. It took the wild fire of an untamed heart seeking something that felt real and true. It took a willingness to live outside every convention that taught me to want something else.

There were moments of pure bliss—hanging off the side of a Southern Pacific train, desert wind rushing through my hair. Watching waves roll off the backs of whales from a fishing boat off the Alaskan coast. Sharing conversations around a campfire that I thought I would always remember. But I wasn't happy.

Fast-forward two decades and that restless, wanderlusty teen had put down roots and was building the life she had once so boldly rebelled against. I had a husband, a successful corporate career, a big house, and a gaggle of girlfriends to drink wine with on the weekends. I had what I was supposed to want. And still I wasn't happy. Not in the way I expected to be. Not in the way that filled my heart and ignited my soul.

Here's what I finally figured out: the cage wasn't the conventional life or the radical one. The cage was living a life that wasn't actually mine. It didn't matter if I was sleeping under a bridge or in a king-sized bed with Egyptian cotton sheets. It didn't matter if I was hitchhiking in the back of a rusty pickup or driving a nice car with heated leather seats. I was still performing. Still pretending. Still living according to a script—sometimes playing the rebel, sometimes acting out the girl boss, but always a movie of someone else's life. I hadn't allowed myself to be fully seen. Not by anyone else, and not even by me.

I was living from urges and inclinations without translating them into something authentic and coherent. I felt the whispers and shouts of what I wanted and how I longed to live, but I kept dancing around the edges. I didn't know my real intention for being here. I didn't know my blueprint. I was just reacting. Performing. Fumbling through trial and error, trying on different costumes and hoping one would finally feel like me. There was nothing wrong with that. It was part of my process, my curriculum, and my journey. It's part of what makes the human experience so compelling—we begin as wide-eyed babies, learning by touching, feeling, and putting things in our mouths. We are meant to learn as we grow. We often discover what we want and need through what deprives us of it.

But it doesn't have to be so hard. It doesn't need to take a lifetime of wading through the muck to finally get clear on what truly matters most...to you. Not what should matter, not what other people want or expect of you, not what society deems right, proper, and successful. But what fulfills and delights *you*.

The struggle has its place. But I'm much happier having made it to the other side. Not because my life is perfect but because I feel alive. I feel peace. When I lay my head on the pillow, I have the sweet smile of someone who self-directed her day. This became possible when I finally understood the difference between broadcasting my authentic signal and adding static to the noise. That's what this book is about. Not whether you should sit in an office or stand in front of a blank canvas. Not which job, relationship, or lifestyle will complete you. It's about something more fundamental: revealing your actual blueprint, clearing the interference, and living in coherence with who you actually are. That is unwavering authenticity.

Because until you do that—until you see yourself clearly and allow yourself to be seen—you can ride all the freight trains in the world or climb all the corporate ladders, and you'll still be in the cage. I spent decades behind those bars. I tried breaking out by going west, then by building corporate success. I tried breaking out through partnership, spiritual seeking, achievement, and surrender. None of it worked because I was trying to break out of the wrong thing.

The cage wasn't any external condition or circumstance. The cage was my unwillingness to embrace the full truth of me and have the courage to express that across every area of my life. The key that unlocked the door wasn't simply another change—moving, divorcing, quitting my job. The key was discovering and then honoring what I truly value, what motivates me at the deepest levels, and how the structure of my life needs to support that. It was coming into coherence in everything I do.

That's the work this book does. It uncovers your untamed truths—what is honest, real, and uncensored. It reveals your Blueprint of Being through your Sovereign Need and most closely held values. I guide you in identifying your Life Intention—not some fixed cosmic destiny but what calls you to mastery and gives your life meaning. You will also architect the Life Design that wholly supports what you want for your life. Through this process, you will finally have language that clearly articulates who you are, what you stand for, and what fulfills you.

With your untamed truths in hand, I show you how to recognize interference—all the ways you've been self-abandoning and self-sabotaging, creating static that weakens your signal. And then

I teach you how to clear that interference and live from unwavering authenticity and coherence instead. Why unwavering? Because coherence demands consistency with your untamed truths, even when those truths disappoint, confuse, or alienate people. It's the willingness to be yourself in the face of every external pressure and temptation—when the voices around you are screaming something else, when staying small would be easier, when your truth makes others uncomfortable. Unwavering authenticity is the antidote to people-pleasing, spiritual bypassing, and anything else asking you to betray yourself. It is the defender of your self-sovereignty.

Now, I need to be honest with you. The path of coherence requires courage. It demands that you take responsibility for your life and make the choices that honor yourself. It requires walking away from comfortable patterns that no longer work and stepping into the unknown. It means getting unflinchingly honest about where you've been performing and self-deceiving and having the guts to stop. It asks that you care more about your happiness than your wounds and fears. This is the reclamation: restoring your wild self—free of conditioning and coercion—to its natural state as the sole author of your life.

This path isn't for everyone. It's for people who want to answer their deepest calls and longings, even if it's scary. It's for the spirits that don't want to stay small and on the sidelines of their own lives. It's for people who love themselves enough to bring their brightest light to the world. If that's you—my sacred rebels and wild hearts—I offer you a hug and a hand. This is the journey of a lifetime. You are freeing what has always yearned to emerge through you—your untamed truths that refused to be silenced.

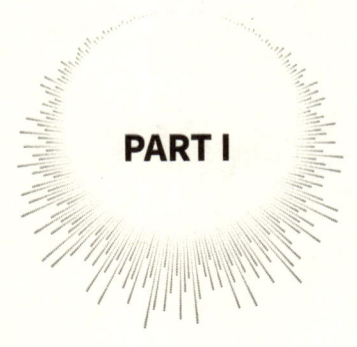

PART I

Recognizing the Untamed Truths of You

1

How Good Can It Get?

You don't need my permission to love your life. But I'm going to give it to you anyway. Because so many of us have doubted and denied our dreams for so long that we no longer trust the yearnings of our hearts. We have absorbed criticisms and cautions from family, friends, and society at large—voices calling our aspirations selfish, unrealistic, or even impossible. The same chorus of voices that say they want the best for us often omit what they really mean. They want the best for us so long as it doesn't create any discomfort for them.

And so, we often develop a complicated relationship with our own nature and desires. We are torn between inspiration and obligation, talents and taking care of others, passion and paying the bills. Though these are often false choices and illusory trade-offs, the worries rattle our minds, warning us of the danger of following our dreams. It can start to feel safer to want nothing. To be satisfied with the scraps of our longings and shrink our own dreams. We become the loudest voice telling ourselves why we can't. We put ourselves in the cage.

I'm not here to shame you for that. I spent a good chunk of my life there. Nor am I here to whip you into a frenzy and push you to blow up your life. No judgment from me if that is what you choose, but this book doesn't prescribe what to do. It invites you to fully express all that you already are. It gives you permission to want what you truly want—not the backup option or scaled-down version, but the vision that expands and electrifies you. I'm not talking about some glorious achievement witnessed by millions, though it could be. I'm talking about the gentle smile, profound peace, and ever-expanding joy of loving your life. Of knowing that you are being and doing what you are here to do.

You get to decide what that looks like. It has to be unapologetically, unabashedly, and unwaveringly yours. It's okay if you can't see it yet. This book is your guide, offering you tools and practices to keep coming back to what matters most. It helps you tell the truth and practice choosing it daily, so you can align with what you actually want. This is the art of self-sovereignty.

Whatever your situation, you can start now. Even the smallest coherent choices build momentum, rewiring your behavior and making the next choice easier and more intuitive. One aligned decision makes the next one feel obvious. You start seeing tangible evidence of your transformation—new people, opportunities, and experiences that actually match who you are. As your life comes into alignment, you won't be so quick to let in what would disrupt it. The coherence itself becomes what you protect.

Your Untamed Truths Framework

Your life can be whatever you want it to be. What's stopping you is interference: all the ways you've been compromising and undermining your truth. This book is your liberation from what has been holding you back. Not by running away from your life but by getting crystal clear on who you are and why you are here, and living it in everything you do.

This framework emerged from my realization that complete coherence is the key to having the life I truly want. After countless retreats, workshops, manifestation books, and meditations, I understood the basic mechanics of personal transformation. I had taken big leaps—changing my life for the better—but a final piece hadn't yet clicked into place. It took a bad breakup for me to finally see the full pattern. From that clarity, all that I learned over years of consciousness studies, psychological self-examination, and ontological training coalesced into this streamlined framework that I now share with you.

This book covers the three important stages of the coherence journey:

1. **Recognizing the Untamed Truths of You** – Clarifying who you are, why you are here, and how you want to live

2. **Seeing the Interference Patterns** – Being honest about where you aren't living your truth

3. **Practicing Coherence and Self-Sovereignty** – Consistently aligning your thoughts, beliefs, behavior, and choices to create a life you love

The first stage builds your map. This map is at the heart of the framework because it reveals what truly matters to you, what you keep coming home to. It becomes your internal navigation system—the compass that makes every decision clearer, every boundary easier to hold, every choice more aligned with who you are. It is not something you pick or wish were true—it is what has always been honest and real at your core.

This map has three components—Blueprint of Being, Life Intention, and Life Design—each reinforcing the others. Your Blueprint of Being is what makes you, you. In sketching your Blueprint, you will understand which of the six Universal Needs for human thriving is your Sovereign Need. Your Sovereign Need is what makes you self-determined and answerable to your inner authority rather than external validation. It is your non-negotiable Need—what you will sacrifice last. Your Sovereign Value directly enables it—without this value, your Sovereign Need cannot exist. This quality, like courage, honesty, or compassion, is yours to embody regardless of circumstances. Beyond the Sovereign Value, you have other values that express who you are when you're living coherently—your value constellation that guides your behavior and helps you recognize alignment.

Your Blueprint of Being offers clues to your Life Intention. Your Life Intention is why you are here and what makes your life meaningful. This isn't a specific job, role, or physical achievement, but what you seek to master. It is your specialization—the theme or lesson you came to understand and embody so thoroughly that you model it for others. Your Life Design is the general specifications that support your Blueprint and Life Intention. It is the structure that they are built on. It includes the nature of your physical environment, how you structure your time, who you surround yourself with, and what you do with your days.

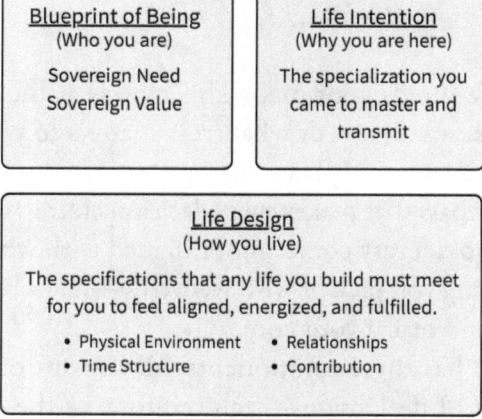

The Untamed Truths Framework

When all three pieces of your map are in harmony—all authentically expressed—you are in the powerful, aligned state of coherence. Authenticity is coherence. Within this Circle of Coherence, everything about you is broadcasting the same clear, authentic signal. In coherence, your creativity freely flows, you recognize aligned opportunities, and you attract people who resonate with the truth of you. You become a beacon for what enhances your life.

Because most of us absorbed the beliefs, opinions, and expectations of others—along with social, cultural, and religious programming—we come to this work not in complete coherence with our authentic selves. We've been performing for approval and acceptance, and placing security above our heart's desires. We've been rationalizing and bypassing, undermining and deceiving ourselves. The second stage reveals where you have been compromising your truth through interference.

Interference kicks you out of the Circle of Coherence in two ways: chasing what isn't yours or undermining what is. Clear the interference and your creative power stops canceling itself out. Your Circle of Coherence becomes its own force field, protecting the authenticity within and repelling what doesn't belong.

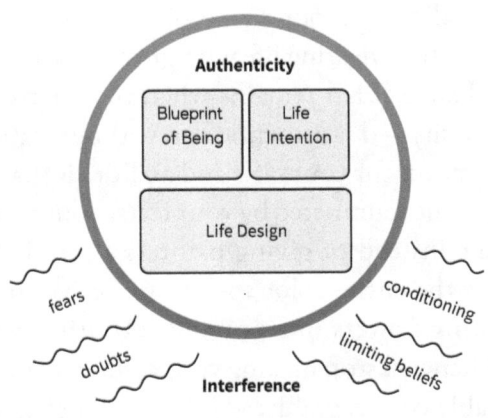

The Circle of Coherence

The third stage is all about putting it into practice. It's about seeing and feeling the interference and making coherent choices anyway. It poses the two questions that will make the biggest difference in your life: "Is it mine?" and "Does it align?" As you start screening your choices based on the answers to those questions, you build your coherence muscle, making the next decision easier. Eventually, choosing what is best for you becomes intuitive, until it is second nature. This is the virtuous cycle your coherence sets in motion, starting with knowing what is authentically yours.

But I don't just drop you off in your new life and speed away. The final part of this book deals with the hard questions: What do you do when you know the coherent choice and still struggle to make it? How do you manage relationships that no longer fit? How do you handle the grief over the life you let go? You'll get concrete tools for making coherent choices in real life, with real constraints and real resistance. I'll help you navigate the chrysalis—that liminal, messy space between dissolution and embodiment.

What Coherence Catalyzes

When you start aligning around who you truly are and what matters most, you start navigating life with greater clarity. That clarity is your natural state, what remains when the interference clears. Coherence is clarity—the authentic you without static.

What this means for your gifts and abilities is that they can be fully expressed, unencumbered by your fears, doubts, and limiting beliefs. It's like instead of giving painters a set of three colors, they can access the entire color spectrum. Or like the difference between planting flowers in a pot and scattering seeds across a fertile field. When you stop making your abilities conform to what feels comfortable or acceptable, you become a clear conduit for the inspiration that naturally wants to flow through you. It isn't just that you will focus, practice more, and naturally improve your craft—your abilities themselves will expand.

Expect to be surprised at how capable, intuitive, and brave you truly are. Your personal power gets amplified because your signal is broadcasting loud and clear. When your thoughts, beliefs, and actions are all pointing in the same direction, all that energy is harnessed toward forward motion. You aren't leaking energy tending to what's dragging behind. Your signal isn't being consumed and canceled out by the static.

You start seeing opportunities you couldn't see before. But more than that, what matches your signal finds you—you become more visible and magnetic. Because you aren't cutting in and out, what's headed your way can lock on, like your phone connecting to a wireless speaker. A popular podcaster sees your video on social media and invites you on his show. Your neighbor inherits a cabin on your favorite lake that she has no use for and sells it to you for cheap. Someone invites a friend to a meeting you're hosting who becomes the love of your life. Or you simply start strumming the guitar and give birth to a beautiful song. Whether anyone bears witness to your experiences or not, when you send out a clear signal, you get a clear response.

Thankfully, this also keeps unwanted things at bay. The people and opportunities that don't match your signal—that are incompatible with your truth—either never cross your path, or you immediately recognize they're not for you. The options that would derail you stop even registering as possibilities. Consider my friend who quit alcohol 15 years ago. He learned to love the peace of his new life more than the chaos of his old. That makes returning to his addiction not a real choice at all. Coherence follows the same path. No drama, no struggle, no guilt—just naturally wanting what is best for you.

As you come into coherence, it's not that everything starts showing up in your life. It's that *your* everything gets a chance to be fully experienced and expressed. With every aligned choice, you say yes to your authentic self. You start trusting your instincts and intuition again. You listen to your heart. You effortlessly choose what honors your highest path—not just what keeps the peace. You allow your life to open as you cultivate what you want to see bloom. This might be a major external change or an internal shift in perspective that lets go of anxiety, stress, or anger. Whatever form it takes, the mark of coherence is how much better you feel about your decisions and circumstances.

Why It Is Worth It

This journey can feel hard at first. Not hard as in running a marathon, but hard because it demands honesty. It is being willing to strip away whatever stories you've told yourself, whatever excuses you've relied on, whatever limitations you've taken as fact. It feels hard because you might realize how entrenched and entangled you are in a life you no longer want. Hard because you know you'll have some difficult decisions to make. Whatever has kept you from standing in your full power and light needs to be let go.

And it is worth it. Think of a time when you made the hard but honest choice. Maybe you left a relationship that was draining you. Maybe you abandoned the degree program you'd invested three years and thousands of dollars in. Maybe you spoke up about corruption or fraud at your company. It may have been scary, sad, and unsettling, but what else did you feel? I'm betting you felt *relief*.

There is tremendous relief in no longer living a charade. Inner conflict—that battle between knowing what is best for you and not doing it—is punishing. Whether it's a subtle nagging or a screaming conscience, being incongruent with the truth we know but won't acknowledge is unbelievably stressful. Violating our core truths can lead to existential anxiety, making us question the roots of who we are and what we stand for, not to mention the toll it takes on our health. Even if it dwells in the dark of our subconscious, the psyche knows and the body keeps score, and they will never stop trying to get our attention. Continuing to ignore it makes it worse, whether that shows up as conflict, emotional crisis, or physical illness.

Admittedly, your relief at finally being honest may not be shared by the people around you. Other people are often invested in our lie for myriad reasons. They might love you and think they know what is best for you. They might seek to save you from the hardships they see ahead. They might be devastated by the thought of losing you, or at least losing the version of you they know.

Though it may be conveyed with anger, shame, or catastrophic negativity, the people who would dissuade you are often trying to protect you because they care about you. But let's be honest—they are also trying to protect themselves. Maybe they see you as a reflection of themselves, and the idea that you would break from the norm threatens their need for group acceptance. Maybe they are worried that as you grow, you will grow apart from them. Or maybe they are terrified that watching you follow your dreams will make it impossible to ignore that they abandoned theirs. If you can do it, so can they, but they know they won't. You waking up makes it harder for them to stay asleep.

They might say you are being selfish. But you know what? Let them say that. Nothing is loving or kind about keeping people trapped in your farce. Nor do we serve anyone by playing along with theirs. They deserve the same fulfillment and satisfaction that we do, even if they never claim it.

When you show up for yourself with courage, you give people permission to do the same. You become the flame lighting another candle. Then that person lights another, and another, until the night sky is ablaze. You serve by modeling what is possible. The people who truly love you will celebrate your joy, even if it makes them nervous. Those who have judged you will perceive that you've discovered something about life still eluding them. That is the spark you ignite.

You don't just fall in love with your life. You show people it is possible to fall in love with theirs. That is one of your many contributions to the world. The things you give up along the way? You find that little was worth having. The crutches that kept you limping along. The nights of mindless TV bingeing, social media scrolling, drunken conversations, and dates with people who make you want to escape to the bathroom and never come back. The days you gave over to the grind that passed in a blur on perpetual repeat. You give up all the things you did to keep up appearances, earn approval, feel safe, and keep yourself small. I had nervous moments standing in the ashes of my former life and nostalgic moments of missing certain people and old times, but the thought of going back to who I was pretending to be was like putting on a wet bathing suit three sizes too small.

Why is the journey worth it? Because your happiness matters. Your fulfillment matters. You deserve joy. You are worthy of the unfathomable exhilaration of discovering all that you are capable of. It is not just about avoiding regret or feeling relief—it is about the bliss of going all in, of finding out how good it can be.

The Ever-Evolving Journey

The goal of embodying your Blueprint of Being, Life Intention, and Life Design isn't arrival, enlightenment, or any fixed state that means you are done. Authentic coherence is a state of being. It is a way of walking through the world in constant creation, moving from one experience to the next and then the next. You're not working toward coherence as a destination. You're learning to be coherent in the journey itself.

This was one of my major shifts. Whatever I wanted at the time became my goalpost for having made it. "It" represented a time and place when the ground would stop shaking beneath me, the pace of change would slow, and I would arrive at a destination where there was no gap between what I wanted and what I had. It was like I saw life as an elevator, where eventually I would reach the top floor and be done. I could kick off my shoes, sip a crisp Sauv Blanc, and eat bonbons until it was time to go.

Every time I thought I had finally attained "it" in life, happiness would eventually give way to dissatisfaction, boredom, or constraint. My disappointment would creep back in with a sigh, starting the cycle anew with the added sense that I was screwing up. If this wasn't it, the real "it" must still be out there behind the prize door I hadn't picked. It was no wonder I wasn't content. I was chasing something that didn't exist—an end to an endless journey.

It finally hit me—the point of my life wasn't to achieve a certain "it" but to realize that *all of this is it*. The messiness, discomfort, longing, and the wonder, excitement, and joy. The struggles and setbacks, as well as the triumphs and thrills. I accepted that my wanting and longing would never cease because it's not supposed to. The question shifted from "What is my vision of the future?" to "What would excite me *now*?"

Fulfillment doesn't have a ceiling—it has expanding horizons. Each dream you achieve expands your capacity for a bigger dream and then an even bigger one. There is no end of the line. We exist to create moment-to-moment, and when we fully embrace that, it becomes our greatest joy. Not for what we get but for who it allows us to be along the way. The shiny stuff with the bells and whistles will come—not as a reward but as a natural consequence of being unwavering in who you are.

What you discover? The coherence itself is what feels good. The creative flow of coherence is the fulfillment. The simple pleasure of living the life you crafted for yourself is the reward, the means and the end. You can take the pressure off yourself to find that one thing you were "supposed" to do or hit the milestone that will show everyone you succeeded. Being true to yourself is the path.

Let me show you what this looks like when it clicks into place. I had thought it would be a big moment of arriving at that top floor that convinced me I had made it. Instead, I had my big moment alone at my dining room table in front of my laptop while writing this book. It came with a full-body rush, almost like chills without being cold. I felt my heart expand and an electric buzz travel through my veins. Tears welled up in my eyes. It all felt so perfect, so enriching, so supportive.

This book became possible when my life became coherent. The book's core framework and the journey it maps entered my awareness nearly fully formed—an already fertilized egg looking for a nurturing space to gestate and come to life. My life was that womb: the open, receptive, and safe space to bring this idea to the world. Because I am living my Life Design, everything was in place to support it. I had the open calendar and free time to be able to focus on it. I had a sunny and creative space conducive to writing for several hours a day. I was single with no one competing for my attention. The writing skills I developed over decades of daily drafting and editing—even if white papers and regulatory filings—meant I instinctively knew how to put the ideas to paper.

It was all there. Like I was directly plugged into my own inspiration. It didn't matter how many hours I spent typing on the computer; I never felt drained. The creative process was generative, not depleting, almost like time had ceased to exist. All the static cleared because my life was so full of what excited me and gave me meaning that there were no gaps to fill. My usual distractions had no crack to sneak through.

In this coherence, I felt the totality of me like I never had before. I experienced more than heightened abilities—I felt my deepest wound close, my darkest fear evaporate, and the ghosts of my self-doubt vanish into the ether. Nothing happened other than my own recognition, my own knowing, my own profound appreciation for myself and my life. Suddenly, how the world responded in terms of book sales, speaking tours, or accolades didn't matter. My joy was happening now.

The moment I had been waiting for wasn't at the end of the journey. The moment *was* the journey, crystallized into conscious knowing. I was already living it. Through that insight, I became free of everything I'd been trying to escape. The invitation became clear: *Why would I want life to settle and stand still when there is infinity to explore?* This is where life gets really fun.

> ### *Untamed Truth*
> Your happiness matters. You came here to model what's possible when you live your fullest expression. Not everyone will support you. You don't need them to. You only need to tell yourself the truth and make one coherent choice, then another. Each aligned choice builds momentum. This is the journey and the joy. Loving your life becomes the invitation of every moment—not a prize awarded at the end. Walking this path will be hard sometimes, but it is so worth it.

2

WHAT MATTERS MOST

I thought I knew who I was. And in many ways, I did. My rebel nature announced itself early. I was the kid who revolted at unfairness and hated being told what to do, who got into punk rock at 13 years old, organized rallies at my high school, and bailed on my first attempt at college to go hitchhike and ride freight trains.

"She's a pistol!" my Nana used to say. Even as a little girl, I played by my own rules. I was strong-willed, independent, and yes, sometimes a brat and trouble-maker. Though I didn't shy away from speaking (okay, sometimes shouting) my truth, my favorite days growing up were the quiet ones. Whether that was reading in my room or twirling blades of grass in a field behind the elementary school, those moments alone were when I met myself.

When we look back at our lives, we can see the common threads. The untamed truth of our being can never be conquered or destroyed—it can only be hidden. Buried underneath the overwhelm, survival strategies, and programming, our pure flame finds ways to shine through. It is more than just our personality—it is a reflection of what matters most.

This chapter gets you going on your Blueprint of Being. It introduces the six Universal Needs for human thriving and explains each of your Blueprint components. Chapter 3 gives you exercises to discover your primary drivers and motivations. They are designed to reveal the patterns already present in your life, what has always been true. The exercises are meant to give you clarity without years of therapy, but they require effort and honesty. Self-knowledge is the foundation embodiment is built on.

But look, I get it. Not everyone loves exercises. And some of you won't feel ready to dive in or will want to read the whole book first. That's fine. While I recommend you do them, you can benefit from this book without putting pen to paper. But if you want to actually apply the coherence practice, you need to know your specific Blueprint. That is what tells you if you are coherent or not. If you skip the exercises, I suggest reading those chapters anyway. You might find that your Blueprint emerges just from the questions and examples. Your intuition is a powerful ally in this work.

The Needs We All Share

You probably know Maslow's Hierarchy of Needs—the pyramid with survival needs at the bottom and self-actualization at the top. It suggests you climb from one level to the next as you meet those needs, until you reach fulfillment. It's a useful model, but more recent developments in human psychology suggest that our internal decision-making is more complex and fluid than an uphill trek from one category of needs to the next. What separates fulfillment from despair isn't external rewards or punishments—it's internal motivation. We aren't just mice seeking cheese and avoiding electric shocks.

The *Self-Determination Theory (SDT)* identifies the innate fundamental needs essential for human motivation and wellbeing. Initially developed in the 1970s by American psychologists Edward Deci and Richard Ryan, the SDT holds that when the base needs of Autonomy, Competence, and Relatedness are met, we flourish. When they're blocked, we suffer. Why is that the case? When the needs are met, your system shifts from survival mode to growth mode. You stop acting from external coercion, obligation, or fear, and start acting from internal alignment. You become the sole author of your life, grounded in your ability to create whatever you need or want.

We're going to take this foundational trio of Autonomy, Competence, and Relatedness and expand it into six Universal Needs that capture the full spectrum of our physical, psychological, and spiritual requirements. These Universal Needs are the conditions that must be present, or at least actively pursued, for you to operate at full power:

- **Autonomy & Agency:** The power to be the author and actor in your own life—your inherent free will

- **Connection & Belonging:** The need for close bonds and inclusion within a community

- **Curiosity & Competence:** The drive to learn, grow, and feel effective in your environment

- **Safety & Security:** The foundational requirement for stability, predictability, and freedom from threat

- **Dignity & Worth:** The need to be witnessed, respected, and acknowledged as having intrinsic value

- **Transcendence & Meaning:** The spiritual drive to find purpose and contribute to something larger than yourself

These drivers determine whether you feel vibrant or barely get through each day. They are the bedrock upon which your personal Blueprint is built. As you'll discover, one of these six—your Sovereign Need—will win out when forced to choose. It is your primary driver—what feels most like you, what motivates you, and where you find fulfillment. Having a Sovereign Need doesn't mean the others aren't important—they are all necessary for wellbeing. You will care about all of them—your Sovereign Need is simply the most non-negotiable. It's what you'll sacrifice last.

Of course, in life-threatening situations, survival instinct takes over—that's biology, not Blueprint. Your Sovereign Need is what you focus on once basic survival is secured. For example, someone with a Sovereign Need of Safety & Security isn't just reacting to immediate threats. They're structuring their entire life around stability—building emergency funds, maintaining set schedules and plans, choosing more secure jobs, preparing for contingencies. Even when not at risk, they prioritize Safety & Security above other Needs.

This is different from someone prioritizing Safety & Security because of past trauma. For many people who experienced instability, poverty, or abuse growing up, the terror of not feeling safe makes Safety & Security dominant. For some, it might be their Sovereign Need—they are energized by being a calming presence for those in chaos, building resilience in their communities, or following their daily routine. For others, it is a baseline condition that must be met for them to explore other Needs, not a source of fulfillment itself. It's a prerequisite, not a driver. Safety & Security stops being sovereign once it is satisfied.

As we work through the Blueprint, I'll call out common scenarios where wounds and trauma responses can confuse what is actually sovereign. You'll learn to separate fear from authentic signal. The truth of you is there, waiting to be revealed.

The One Need That Rules Them All

Your Sovereign Need is the one that speaks to the most authentic truth of you and is at the core of how you show up in the world. It is why you are the way you are. Your Sovereign Need is the source of your greatest joy and fulfillment when met, and the sharpest, unrelenting pain when violated.

Consider my dear friend who left California and built a beautiful homestead with her husband in a more affordable area on the East Coast. The plan was to have their daughters follow and create a safe haven should things fall apart. But the daughters didn't like the area and went back to California. For two years, my friend made it work, but it never felt like home. The homestead sat vacant while she and her husband spent most of their time back in California. When talking to my friend about what to do, I asked her, "If you're safe at your property but can't reach your daughters and don't know if they're alive, which matters more to you?" She teared up. The answer was obvious.

My friends had built their lives around Safety & Security, driven by legitimate concerns, but also by worries of "What if?" Because what was sovereign was their connection with their daughters, no amount of physical security could compensate for the loss of being near them. The fear had overtaken the signal of true joy. The homestead—the ultimate expression of Safety & Security—felt empty without the people who made Safety meaningful. That's how you know what's truly sovereign: it's what makes everything else matter.

This is what a Sovereign Need does: it reveals itself when everything else falls away. It's what you cannot violate and still feel like yourself and still be happy. It's the need that, when unmet, makes everything else feel hollow, no matter how well other areas of your life are going. But as critical as your Sovereign Need is as a guidepost, it is not a dogma by which to judge yourself or others. There is a difference between honoring your Sovereign Need and making it a tyrant. Unwavering doesn't mean unkind or intolerant. You can honor your Need by waiting until the right time to address something or gathering more data. It doesn't have to be a confrontation, nor are others obligated to acknowledge your Need. The point is to be aware of what is unfolding and respond consciously and authentically.

There's usually wiggle room where we can shift and flex to honor our Sovereign Need while staying authentic. For example, if your Sovereign Need is Dignity & Worth and a partner makes an insensitive joke about your weight gain, you might be satisfied with a simple apology or even be willing to let it go because it wasn't malicious. On the other hand, if your partner is continuously belittling and shaming you for your weight, you are never going to feel okay about that. You can lie to yourself and make excuses, but that nagging voice inside you will get louder until you do something to reaffirm your Dignity & Worth.

That said, some things are an automatic "no." If someone tries to override my Agency by lying and manipulating me, they're out. If someone harms me—not just hurts my feelings but actually does me (or others) serious harm—buh-bye. If someone violates another's right to life or bodily autonomy, they are not welcome in my world. I might have compassion for whatever drove them to it, but people who willingly and wantonly violate the Universal Needs of others have no place in my life. My dignity demands that.

So far, we've talked about the six Universal Needs we all share as humans and how there is one Sovereign Need that comes first for you. Now we are going to talk about the Sovereign Value that enables your Sovereign Need to exist.

The Partner You Need

Your Sovereign Value is paramount because without it, you couldn't fulfill your Sovereign Need. Let me walk you through the logic, using myself as an example. My Sovereign Need is Autonomy & Agency. It is my power to create my life according to my will, wants, and wildest desires. It is the freedom to be me across all areas of my life and make my own decisions. What is necessary for me to live a life according to my dreams and convictions? Courage. Autonomy & Agency is not possible without it. What I want for my life demands bravery.

Living your truth often means facing fears—the fear of rejection, failure, opposition, and entering the uncertain and unknown. It can mean saying things that people would rather not hear, crafting an unconventional life, and standing alone in your integrity. Without courage, you can be swayed and directed by external forces, like your parents and friends, societal and cultural expectations, and anyone else threatened by what you stand for. Without courage, you can talk yourself out of your biggest dreams.

In other examples, someone with a Sovereign Need of Connection & Belonging might have a Sovereign Value of compassion. Without compassion, genuine connection isn't possible. Compassion creates an emotionally safe space where authentic relating can happen without judgment. It could also be transparency, as true belonging requires the courage to be clear in who you are rather than performing for acceptance.

Someone with a Sovereign Need of Dignity & Worth may have a Sovereign Value of honesty. Without the willingness to tell themselves and others the truth—especially uncomfortable truths about what they will and won't accept—dignity erodes through silent accommodation and pretense. Honesty is what makes self-respect possible. Self-trust might be another. Without confidence in their own judgment and the willingness to act on it, they become dependent on external validation and vulnerable to manipulation.

Sovereign Values for Safety & Security include preparation, reliability, and consistency. Preparation means anticipating needs and risks before they arise. Reliability creates the predictable patterns that allow you to trust your environment and yourself. Consistency establishes the stable foundations and routines that keep chaos at bay, creating the bedrock of safety that allows you to live rather than just survive.

While there are many Sovereign Values that could map to a Sovereign Need, the one that is most yours will feel foundational. It's the value that shows up repeatedly in your hardest decisions, the one you've had to embody every time you've honored what matters most. When you finally articulate it, you should feel a sense of recognition, maybe even relief: "Yes, this is what makes everything else possible for me."

But here's something to watch for: sometimes what you defend most vigorously and react to most strongly when challenged isn't your Sovereign Value, but a protective mechanism rooted in fear and childhood wounds. I'll give you an example. For years, I hated when people insulted my intelligence—whether by lying, trying to manipulate me, or anything else that triggered that "Do you think I'm a frickin' idiot?!" response. It might seem like intelligence is my Sovereign Value, but it was part of how I learned to feel safe. If I could see through lies, predict what was coming, and stay several steps ahead, I couldn't be blindsided or controlled. It was all about gaining the upper hand so I wouldn't get hurt. Once I saw this clearly, I stopped defending my intelligence and allowed it to simply be a trait I possess, like having green eyes. I stopped weaponizing it and let it serve what matters, instead of defending it at all costs.

Here's the difference between protective mechanisms and your Sovereign Value. Protective mechanisms are constructed from fear and designed to keep us safe from perceived threats. When they kick in, we feel highly defensive—maybe even entering fight-or-flight—and contracted. We try to prove ourselves, needing others to validate us so we feel safe again. In contrast, your Sovereign Value should feel like something that enables your best self, not just your defended self. It is freedom, not armor. Your Sovereign Value emerges naturally when the protective strategies fall away. It keeps reasserting itself no matter what you layer on top of it.

Your Value Constellation

Becoming crystal clear about your Sovereign Need and Sovereign Value gives you the foundation of your Blueprint. But you have other values that matter to you—qualities you embody, standards you hold, ways you show up when you're being authentically you. They're expressions of your coherence, when there is no gap between who you are on the inside and how you show up on the outside. When you live coherently, you are living with integrity. Coherence is integrity with self. Life becomes easier because you have an operating manual for what you have already decided is important to you.

For example, I value kindness and compassion. They guide how I show up in relationships and how I treat myself. They also act as a filter for how I express my Sovereign Need and Value. For example, when supporting people through a difficult time, kindness and compassion often mean listening while refusing to see them as victims incapable of change or having what they want. I won't nod along to a narrative that positions them as powerless and the situation as hopeless. To me, an action is not truly kind if it undermines a person's Agency. Compassion is not seeing someone as broken but acknowledging the struggle of being human. If my candor makes me not nice or empathetic in someone else's eyes, I'm okay with that. I have the courage to be coherent with who I am. At the end of the day, I am the one who must feel good about my actions. My values are my guide to feeling good.

You'll identify your value constellation in the next chapter's exercises. For now, just know that these values matter—they inform your decisions, guide your behavior, and help you recognize alignment and misalignment. But they work differently from your Sovereign pair. Violating your Sovereign Need often feels like a dealbreaker or crisis. Violating your other values registers as misalignment—worth noticing, worth addressing, but not catastrophic. But before we dive into your specific Blueprint of Being, let's recap what we have covered. The table below summarizes each component of your Blueprint.

Component	Definition
Universal Needs	The inherent psychological and spiritual requirements of all humans, necessary to sustain life, foster growth, and prevent suffering.
The Sovereign Need	The most vital energetic driver for an individual. When forced to choose, this need trumps all others. It defines the individual's primary mode of engagement with the world.
Sovereign Value	The value that most directly enables the Sovereign Need. Without it, the Sovereign Need can't be met and the entire Blueprint is compromised.
Value Constellation	The other values that express who you are when living coherently. These emerge naturally from coherence rather than being required for it.

Summary of Blueprint Components

The next chapter guides you through three exercises designed to clarify your Sovereign Need and Sovereign Value—the foundation of your Blueprint. You'll also identify your value constellation, the other values that express who you are when you're living coherently. There is a supplemental exercise in the Appendix, should you want additional input. These exercises are available in a printable workbook format for free at: www.youruntamedtruths.com.

Untamed Truth

Your Blueprint of Being is more than your character or personality—it is what you hold sacred. It is what you cannot compromise and still feel like you. Your Sovereign Need and Sovereign Value aren't chosen or cultivated—they are what was always there beneath the static.

3

Sketching Your Blueprint

········✵········

I'm not going to lie. Clarity on my Blueprint came through an intense reckoning that stripped away every protective layer I'd built and every defense mechanism I hid behind. I was laid completely bare. It was raw, uncomfortable, and what I needed to truly shut down my old patterns. While there can be benefits in stepping into the fire like that, there are gentler ways that are more of an unearthing than a dynamite blast. Your Blueprint has always been there, waiting to be seen. What matters most is already asserting itself in how you make decisions, what brings you alive, and what you simply cannot tolerate. The work is recognizing what's always been calling you home.

What follows are different entry points into your Blueprint based on the different ways people process information. The exercises are approaching the same answers from distinct angles. Because insights often emerge through iteration, I encourage you to take the time to sit with them. Your first pass might not be your final answer. That's not getting it wrong—it's the discovery process. If it isn't clear at this stage, don't worry. As you move through Life Intention and Life Design in the coming chapters, your Blueprint will continue to come into focus. What matters now is getting close enough that you have a base for what we'll explore next.

Alternatively, you might have looked at the list of Universal Needs and said, "That's it!" I encourage you to go through the exercises anyway. Not as a challenge to your intuition, but because the clarity you feel at confirming what matters to you will be helpful and confidence-building. It's also possible that you learn something new about yourself or find a new way to succinctly summarize what makes you tick. Remember: this isn't about picking the answer your ego wants but what speaks to the untamed truths of you.

If this starts to feel like a lot, know that this chapter is the heavy lifting. The rest of the work builds on this foundation. So grab your notebook and let's dive in. Again, if you would prefer to do these exercises in a printable workbook format, with space to fill in the blanks, head to www.youruntamedtruths.com and download the free PDF.

1 – What Your Body Tells You

Your body is a powerful messenger—trust it.

Part A: Start with expansion

Think about the last time you felt genuinely alive and sublimely content—not performing happiness, not Instagram-worthy photo ops, but that deep sense of "Yes, this is it." What comes to mind for me is having dinner at an adorable outdoor café I stumbled upon while road-tripping. The sun was out, the menu had the fresh, delicious, and veggie-centered food I love, and a band was playing my favorite jazz. I sipped on a fruity Pinot Grigio from a local vineyard without a care in the world.

In that moment, I absolutely loved my life. My heart swelled, my smile radiated, and I wiped away tears of gratitude and joy before they fell on my salted caramel brownie. Everything I had been through was worth it for that moment of freedom and pure satisfaction.

What about you? When do you love your life the most? When are you most proud of yourself? You might think of your perfect day. Or perhaps a conversation where you felt completely yourself, a difficult decision you made that felt unmistakably right, or a moment when you stood your ground on something important. It might be something you couldn't wait to tell your mom or best friend or an experience that was so gratifying you felt like your life could end tomorrow and you'd die happy. You can write this down or hold it in your mind.

Notice what's happening in your body right now as you recall it. Is there a sense of opening? Lightness? Energy moving through you? Are you smiling? That's expansion. That's your system saying, "This is aligned, this is you." The first two questions address the qualities and feelings that made it meaningful. The next two questions focus on what you did or honored within yourself that made the experience stand out.

- What made this moment so powerful was:

- The most essential element that lit me up was:

- The way I showed up in this moment was:

- What I honored about myself was:

Part B: Move to contraction

Now think about a time when you didn't honor something important to you—not a simple mistake, but a moment when you knew better and did it anyway, or didn't do something you knew you should have.

Vivid in my mind is driving across town at 9 p.m. to see a guy who had been breadcrumbing me for months. He'd blow me off, go silent for weeks, then send a playful enough text to keep me on the hook. Being my first romance post-divorce, it was a daily struggle to get over him. It was finally working—and then I got his text asking me if I wanted to come over.

Before I could finish yelling, "Are you f-ing kidding me?" I was texting him back and racing to take a shower. As I was driving over there, I half expected a tree to fall in front of the road as divine intervention to stop me from doing something every fiber of my being said was stupid. Not stupid because he was dangerous or I wouldn't have a fun time, but because it would erase the progress I made getting over him, affirming my worth, and protecting my dignity. I felt pathetic in my lack of self-control and self-respect.

What about you? When have you felt that sick, hollow feeling of betraying what is best for you? It might be when you said yes when you really meant no, or when you knew the right thing to do but couldn't bring yourself to do it. Maybe you stayed quiet instead of speaking up, acted in ways that hurt people, or compromised in ways that left you feeling diminished. Not just disappointed—smaller.

These often show up as moments that still make you angry years later, situations where you felt powerless or trapped, or times you betrayed yourself to keep the peace. Notice the sensation in your body right now as you think about that moment. The tightness. The contraction. Maybe it's in your chest, your throat, your gut. It's that icky, uneasy feeling that is hard to shake. For me, it usually feels like someone is sitting on my chest, making it hard to breathe. Stay with that feeling for a moment—your body is trying to tell you something important. The first two questions target what bothered you the most about the situation. The next two questions target how you felt about how you showed up.

- What bothered me most about this situation was:

- What was missing, denied, or violated that created this pain was:

- The thing I did that keeps gnawing at me is:

- What I betrayed in myself was:

Part C: What this reveals about your Sovereign Need

Let me show you how I worked through my moments first, then you'll do the same. Looking at what made my moment in the café so powerful, I see several Universal Needs being met. The novelty and exploration satisfied my Curiosity & Competence. The beauty and synchronicity gave me a sense of Transcendence & Meaning. Being able to handle the unknown and provide for myself addressed Safety & Security and built my Dignity & Worth.

But here's what really mattered: I made every choice that led to that moment. I chose to leave my career. I chose to get in the car without a destination. No one was directing me, accommodating me, or needing me to be anywhere else. The fact that I was alone wasn't a compromise—it was essential to the perfection of the moment.

What made my heart swell wasn't the meal or the music or even the many uncanny synchronicities—it was the joy of freedom and living according to my own compass. It was letting my intuition guide me to exactly what I wanted, down to one of my favorite desserts. I got a literal taste of what was possible for the rest of my life. That was Autonomy & Agency asserting itself as what matters most to me.

I initially wondered if Transcendence & Meaning was sovereign, given how blissful the experience felt. I realized that Autonomy & Agency and Transcendence & Meaning are intricately linked, but it is choosing Autonomy & Agency that gives me that deep sense of meaning. Sometimes what feels meaningful is the result of honoring your Sovereign Need, not the Need itself. If multiple Needs seem equally important, ask: "Which one is the cause and which is the effect?" The cause is your Sovereign Need.

When I look at my contraction moment with the breadcrumbing guy, the same need for Autonomy & Agency shows up—but violated. I wanted to protect my progress and dignity and demonstrate my growth, but I overrode my own knowing. In a blow to my self-sovereignty, I felt powerless to step out of my old pattern and choose what was best for me over what felt good in the moment. I put myself at his whim, choosing compulsion and self-abandonment over conscious choice. What bothered me the most was that I lacked the courage and conviction to honor my own truth. This pattern—expansion when I honor my power to choose and act according to my truth, contraction when I betray it—reveals Autonomy & Agency as my Sovereign Need.

Your Turn

Look at your own expansion and contraction moments. Which Universal Need is being honored or violated? Don't overthink this—go with your gut. Here are the Universal Needs for easy reference.

- **Autonomy & Agency**: Your power to choose and act according to your own truth

- **Connection & Belonging**: Close bonds and feeling part of something

- **Curiosity & Competence**: Learning, growing, feeling capable

- **Safety & Security**: Stability, predictability, freedom

from threat

- **Dignity & Worth**: Being respected and valued for who you are

- **Transcendence & Meaning**: Purpose and contribution to something larger

The Need that shows up in both your expansion (when honored) and contraction (when violated) is pointing toward your Sovereign Need.

- In my expansion moment, the Universal Need being honored was:

- In my contraction moment, the Universal Need being violated was:

When Different Sovereign Needs Show Up

Sometimes the expansion and contraction moments show different Sovereign Needs. For example, your expansion moment might involve learning something new (Curiosity & Competence), while your contraction involves Dignity & Worth. But when you dig deeper, you discover that the excitement of learning and exploring only becomes possible when you're not defending your dignity from threats. The joy comes from deeming yourself worthy of the experiences you want to have and not being shamed or belittled by others. This is the distinction—when your Sovereign Need is met, you can enjoy the other Needs. When it is violated, the other Needs are either impossible or unfulfilling. Your Sovereign Need is the prerequisite.

If different Needs showed up for you, ask yourself: "Which Need is the baseline condition that enables other Needs? Which Need, if met, would truly light me up versus just make me feel safe?" If it isn't clear, don't worry. You'll gather more data in the next exercise and Exercise 3 has additional prompts to see what is sovereign. Note both Needs and keep moving forward.

Part D: What this reveals about your Sovereign Value

Let's also consider the enabling values. Look back at your expansion moment. How did you show up? What quality or way of being made that moment possible? In my café moment, the quality that made it all possible was courage—the courage to leave my career, to get in the car without a destination, to trust myself in the unknown. Without courage, I couldn't have accessed that Autonomy. Courage is my closest-held value for myself.

For you, it might have been honesty, presence, compassion, openness, or discernment. There are no wrong answers. Write down the quality you embodied that made your expansion moment possible.

- The quality I embodied that made my expansion possible was:

Now look at your contraction moment. What quality were you unable to access? What would it have taken to honor your Sovereign Need in that situation? In my breadcrumbing guy moment, I lacked the courage to choose what was best for me over what felt good in the moment. The same quality that created my expansion was absent in my contraction. Write down the quality you needed but couldn't access in your contraction moment.

- In my contraction moment, the quality I couldn't access was:

If the same quality shows up in both—present in expansion, absent in contraction—that's likely pointing toward your Sovereign Value. Hold onto this. Exercise 2 will give you more data and Exercise 3 will pull it together.

2 – What Conflicts Reveal

Conflict is clarifying. What can't you compromise?

Part A: The crucible of choice

Life sometimes puts us in positions where two important Needs come into direct conflict and we can only honor one. These moments strip away what we think matters and reveal what we cannot live without. Think of one or more times when you had to choose between two important things, where honoring one meant sacrificing the other, at least in the near term.

This conflict showed up for me when debating whether to quit my corporate job. The two needs in conflict were Safety & Security and Autonomy & Agency. The security I'd spent 15+ years building on one side and my freedom and self-determination on the other. Write down the two Universal Needs that were in direct conflict for you. This might look like staying in a secure job versus pursuing a dream, being authentic versus maintaining a relationship, or honoring your boundaries versus others' approval.

- The two Needs that conflicted were:

I chose Autonomy & Agency. Staying felt unbearable because it meant managing and controlling variables to feel safe instead of actually living. It meant confining myself to someone else's definition of success. I imagined myself on my deathbed full of regrets at the life I didn't have the courage to choose. That terrified me more than anything. Which one did you choose?

- The Need I chose was:

What made the alternative unbearable? Not just uncomfortable or difficult but devastating. What would you have had to give up about yourself? What would have died inside you? Be specific about why the alternative felt like a betrayal of something essential.

- What made the other option unbearable was:

Part B: What qualities made that choice possible?

For me, it was courage. The same quality that had me heading west with a backpack as a teenager showed up again—courage to walk away from security, to face uncertainty, to trust that whatever came next would be more aligned with who I am. Courage enabled me to honor my Autonomy & Agency even when the logical, sensible choice was to stay.

For your pivotal choice, what quality did you have to embody to honor the need you chose? What made it possible to act despite the cost? Write it down.

- The primary quality that enabled the choice was:

Other qualities play a supporting role. I also needed honesty—brutal honesty with myself about what I wanted versus what looked good on paper. I needed self-trust—knowing that I could figure things out and create my way into or out of any situation, that I'd landed on my feet before and would again. And I needed integrity—the refusal to keep performing a version of success that had never truly satisfied me. What additional qualities supported your decision-making?

- The additional qualities that supported my decision-making were:

Part C: What this reveals about your Sovereign Need

If you've made similar choices multiple times—consistently prioritizing the same Need even in different contexts—that need is likely your Sovereign Need. Looking back, I can see this pattern everywhere. That's how I know Autonomy & Agency is sovereign for me. Not because security or achievement don't matter, but because I cannot compromise my Autonomy & Agency without feeling like I'm betraying myself at the deepest level. That restlessness, that disappointment, that interminable gnawing of knowing I'm settling—that's what shows up when I try to confine myself to anyone else's vision of what my life should be.

Remember my friends with the homestead? Their decisions suggested Safety & Security as their Sovereign Need. But meeting Safety & Security wasn't fulfilling by itself. When forced to choose between their homestead and proximity to their daughters, Connection won. The pattern wasn't in the choices they'd been making from fear—it was in the choice they made from truth. When you take away everything else and ask "What can I not live without?" the answer reveals what's Sovereign.

Now look at your own choice through this lens. Which Need were you choosing *toward* versus which were you choosing *away from*? Sometimes we organize our entire lives around avoiding pain rather than pursuing what makes life meaningful. The Need you are willing to sacrifice security, comfort, or approval for—that's usually your Sovereign Need. The Need you're grinding yourself down to maintain? That might be fear masquerading as necessity.

Look at your life more broadly. Do you see this pattern repeating? Have you consistently chosen one Need over others when forced to pick? The Need you chose—especially if you've chosen it multiple times across different contexts—is likely your Sovereign Need. Write it down.

- The Universal Need I repeatedly chose was:

3 – Assembling The Blueprint

You've gathered data from your body and your choices. Now let's put it all together. This isn't about getting it perfect—aim for clear enough to be useful. Your Blueprint will continue to sharpen as you make your way through this book and as you apply it. There is an additional exercise in the Appendix that finds your non-negotiable breaking point if you want further clarification before proceeding.

Step 1: Declare your Sovereign Need

First, review the exercises for the Need that showed up most consistently across your expansion, contraction, and choice moments (and breaking point if you completed the Appendix exercise). If you feel the truth of your Sovereign Need, skip ahead to "Your Sovereign Need declaration."

Reconciling Multiple Needs

If different Needs showed up in your expansion versus your contraction/choice moments, you're likely seeing the difference between your Sovereign Need and what it enables. This is common and reveals something important about how your Needs interact. Let's figure out which is which. Answer these questions:

1. In my expansion moment, if [contraction Need] had been violated, would the core of what made that moment meaningful still be there?

Example: "In my joyful learning moment, if someone had been belittling me (Dignity violated), would the joy of learning itself still be there, or would the belittling make learning impossible?" If the joy of learning would evaporate, then Dignity & Worth is Sovereign.

2. Which Need, when met, creates the conditions for the other Need to flourish?

Example: Someone needs to feel Dignity before they can risk vulnerability in Connection. Dignity enables Connection; Connection doesn't enable Dignity. Dignity is Sovereign.

3. If I could only have one Need met for the rest of my life, which would I choose? And which Need, when completely absent, makes life feel not worth living?

Example: If you could never have Connection & Belonging again versus never achieving Curiosity & Competence. Which absence is intolerable? The Need whose absence is intolerable—that's your Sovereign Need. It is what you sacrifice last.

Remember that all the Universal Needs matter for human well-being. You might have a Need that is a very close second. In my experience, there is one that you will defend over all others, but if two Needs feel equally essential at this point, you can test them both as you proceed.

Your Sovereign Need declaration

"My Sovereign Need is _____ because when I look at my expansion moments, my deepest pain, and my hardest choices, this is the Need that consistently defines what I cannot compromise and what makes me feel most alive."

You'll know you've found your Sovereign Need when reading the statement feels like coming home to yourself. Like my friend who returned to California to be with her daughters, you might feel that recognition viscerally—tears welling up when someone finally names what has always mattered most.

Step 2: Declare your Sovereign Value

Your Sovereign Value is what enables your Sovereign Need to exist. Without it, the Need collapses, like a building without a foundation. It's also what ensures your Need can never truly be taken away. It is a way of being that satisfies the Need from the inside out.

A) Identify candidate values

Look back at the qualities you identified in Exercises 1 and 2. These were how you showed up in expansion moments, what you couldn't access in contraction moments, and what made your pivotal choice possible. These qualities aren't aspirational virtues—they're the ways of being that made honoring your Sovereign Need possible. They reveal what you value most about your character. Write down the three to five that feel most essential. Now we'll identify which quality is so foundational that without it, your Sovereign Need cannot exist. That's your Sovereign Value.

B) Test each value

Test each value against your Sovereign Need using these two questions:

- *Could I have my [NEED] without [VALUE]?*

If yes → It's not your Sovereign Value, but might be part of your value constellation.
If no → It's a candidate for your Sovereign Value. Move to the second question.

- *If I have [VALUE], can my [NEED] exist, even if everything else is taken away?*

If yes → This is your Sovereign Value.
If no → It's not your Sovereign Value.

Let me show you how this works with my Sovereign Need and Value.

Could I have Autonomy & Agency without courage?

No. Without courage, I'd be paralyzed by fear of consequences, unable to choose according to my truth, and controlled by others' expectations. Courage is what enables me to act on my autonomy. Contrast this with kindness. I could make choices and act on my truth even if I weren't particularly kind. Autonomy doesn't require kindness to exist.

If I have courage, can my Autonomy & Agency exist, even if everything else is taken away?

Yes. Because Autonomy & Agency isn't about my external circumstances; it's about my internal free will. If I have the courage to choose my own attitude and my own truth, I remain internally autonomous even in a prison cell. Courage is my Sovereign Value because it is the one thing no one can take from me that keeps my Autonomy & Agency intact.

Now test your values. For example:

If your Sovereign Need is **Connection & Belonging**:
- *Could I have deep connection without compassion?* No. True connection requires us to open our hearts to each other without judgment and care about their wellbeing.

- *If I have compassion, can my Connection & Belonging exist, even if everything else is taken away?* Yes. When I am deeply compassionate, I am connected to the human experience and at peace with myself. I belong wherever I am because my heart is open.

If your Sovereign Need is **Dignity & Worth**:
- *Could I have dignity without integrity?* No. Worth requires living in alignment with your truth.

- *If I have integrity, can my Dignity & Worth exist, even if everything else is taken away?* Yes. If you know you have acted with total integrity, your internal sense of worth cannot be touched by the opinions or mistreatment of others.

If your Sovereign Need is **Curiosity & Competence**:
- *Could I grow and learn without openness?* No. Development requires being willing to not know and change your mind.

- *If I have openness, can my Curiosity & Competence exist, even if everything else is taken away?* Yes. An open mind finds a lesson in every obstacle and growth in every failure. As long as you remain open, you are constantly evolving, regardless of your environment.

If you're torn between two Sovereign Values, which one made the pivotal choice from Exercise 2 possible? Which one is the foundation and which one is built on top of it? Your Sovereign Value is what everything else requires.

Something else to consider: You might recognize that a value you rely on heavily—perhaps courage, discernment, or self-reliance—was developed as a survival response to trauma. You might think, "This isn't authentically me; this is who I had to become."

Here's what I've learned: The need for the protective mechanism came from trauma, but the capacity to embody that value was always yours. Trauma didn't create your courage—it revealed it. It demanded that you access something that was already there. The question isn't: "Did trauma shape this?" but "Does this value still serve me now?" If courage still enables your Sovereign Need even when you're safe, if it shows up in your expansion moments and not just your survival moments, if you choose it rather than being forced into it—it's authentically yours. You don't have to discard something powerful just because you discovered it through hardship.

However, if a value only shows up when you're in threat mode, if it feels exhausting rather than enlivening, if you'd drop it the moment you felt safe—that's a protective mechanism, not your Sovereign Value.

C) Your Sovereign Value declaration

After testing your values, which one passed both tests? That's your Sovereign Value. Complete this statement:

"My Sovereign Value is _____ because without it, my Sovereign Need of _____ cannot exist. This quality is what enables me to honor what matters most."

Step 3: Identify your value constellation

Your Sovereign Need and Value are your foundation—what you cannot compromise. But you're more than just those two pieces. You have other values that guide how you show up, help you recognize misalignment before it becomes a crisis, and express who you are when living coherently. These don't need the same rigorous testing—just honest acknowledgment.

The other qualities from your exercises that didn't become your Sovereign Value still matter—they're how you express yourself when coherent. Write down the values that speak to how you see your authentic self.

- The values that express who I am are:

Step 4: Your complete Blueprint statement

Now bring it all together in one clear declaration. If you're not 100% certain about your Sovereign Need or Sovereign Value yet, that's fine. Write your best current understanding. As you move through the rest of this book and start living from it, you'll get clarity on whether you need to adjust. The goal right now is "close enough to be useful," not "perfect forever."

My Blueprint of Being

My Sovereign Need is:
My Sovereign Value is:
My value constellation includes:

This is my Blueprint of Being—the untamed truth of who I am when the conditioning, fear, and performance fall away, and I am unwaveringly authentically me.

4

What You Came to Master

When I left my corporate career in 2021, I went through an uncomfortable period of adjusting to the freedom I had created in my life. I was still operating under old programming that tied productivity, achievement, and success to my worth. Frankly, I was also worried about my net worth. After over 15 years of receiving a salary every two weeks, not knowing where my money would come from was scary. And so, I went looking for my next big thing, believing my purpose was about doing something helpful that I could be paid for. Unnerved by the shaky ground beneath me, this search was my way of trying to put certainty and stability back in my life, justified by a desire to be of service.

Like a lot of people, I tried to make a business out of my spiritual awakening. Specifically, I decided to be a life coach. Sound familiar? Over several months, I enrolled in coach training, hired a holistic business coach, developed my signature program, and put it all out on a pretty website. I literally jumped for joy when I signed my first client, believing that I had just walked through the door to my amazing new life. Only it didn't feel amazing.

It didn't take long for the excitement and motivation I felt in building the business to fade. It wasn't just discouragement from a slow start, but a creeping suspicion that I didn't actually want to live the vision I had painted for myself. The prospect of strangers booking my time or spending hours online hustling to find clients sank my spirit. I was just a consultant by another name, still trading hours for dollars.

The untamed truth I finally had to face? I love my life the most when my day is completely open for my own exploration. What feeds my soul is being able to pursue whatever lights me up. During one of my long solo strolls, I realized that my awakening was for me, to bring me to greater understanding, not to keep me stuck in old ways of work dressed up as a spiritual calling. It was to free me from all beliefs that limited my potential, including the productivity trap and the idea that there was one specific thing that I was supposed to do as my "purpose." My actual Life Intention wasn't a service I provide, like being a coach, healer, or writer, but how I live my life. That distinction—between what you do and who you are—is what this chapter is about.

Your Life Intention isn't a profession, job title, or business venture. It isn't a role, like mom, dad, caretaker, or cheerleader. It is what you seek to experience and embody in this life. It is what you came to master and transmit to others. Think of it as your specialization—where you cultivate and hone your expertise, learning your domain so deeply and from so many angles that you become it. Not just understand it but embody and emanate it.

Your Life Intention is why you are here. It is what you want to do with the opportunity of this life, the personal challenge that calls to you, and what will fulfill you. Like your needs and values, you don't find it—you name it, say yes to it, and practice it. You don't pick it—you are it.

Whether you believe that "came here to master" means your soul chose it, your genes predict it, or your childhood shaped it doesn't matter. The pattern is there. The question is whether you'll recognize it and align with it or keep pretending it is something else. The only thing you really need to believe is that you have a choice. To quote poet Mary Oliver: "Tell me, what is it you plan to do with your one wild and precious life?"

In this chapter, we'll explore how to recognize your Life Intention—not through seeking and grasping but through noticing what's been guiding you all along through your passions, talents, and skills.

The Clues in Your Blueprint

Your Life Intention is the calling that keeps calling, the dream that lives in your heart, the longing that will not relent. Like an invisible hand, it pulls you back—again and again—to what will fulfill you. It reveals itself through your Sovereign Need, in the capabilities you've built, and in the patterns that keep showing up across your life. It is the reason you have developed the skills, gifts, talents, passions, and resources you have. Everything about you is designed to help you live your Life Intention. You are simply recognizing what has always been true and what you have been preparing for—typically over years—even if it is only clear in hindsight.

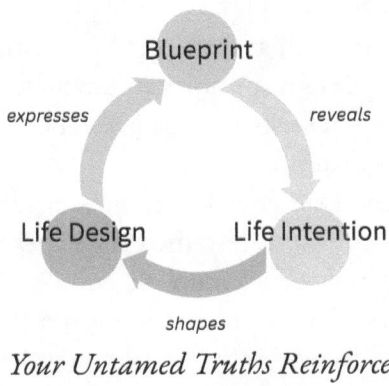

Your Untamed Truths Reinforce Each Other

Your Life Intention is your wound and your medicine, your pain and your passion. For example, which Universal Need torments me most when suppressed and lights me up most fully when honored? Autonomy & Agency. Courage is the Sovereign Value that makes it possible for me. What would excite and challenge someone who wants to be so completely free, so radically self-sourced that their life becomes an invitation and inspiration for others to claim their own limitless freedom?

Liberation from every constraint.

You start to see how it is all interwoven. I cannot serve liberation if I am dependent, restricted, and controlled. I cannot model freedom if I abdicate responsibility for my choices or fail to take accountability for my actions. I simply wouldn't have the passion and energy to serve and sustain this goal if it weren't part of who I am at the most fundamental level. I cannot thrive if that Sovereign Need isn't met because I can't fulfill my Life Intention and vice versa.

Your Sovereign Need and Life Intention are the same core truth of you, expressed in different ways. Your Sovereign Value is that same truth as an embodied quality. Your constellation of other values is what brings it to life in your actions. Your skills and talents are that truth as developed capacities and abilities. Everything in your design supports what you wanted to master. Everything about you seeks to broadcast the same clear signal. That is coherence in action.

This is why knowing your Intention transforms everything. One workshop participant described the experience of naming her Life Intention as feeling "complete, empowered, and fueled." When you stop seeking a purpose as the one specific thing you were "meant" to do and recognize the signal you've been transmitting all along, everything you've built and everything you are suddenly makes sense. This is why there are no wasted experiences. Even if you didn't realize it at the time, so much of what you went through was preparation for what would come next. Once you recognize the specialization you came to master, you can tune every aspect of your life to that same note. Not through force but through removing what's out of tune.

My coaching endeavor wasn't failure—it was feedback. It showed me the difference between force and flow, fear and coherence. It unearthed limiting beliefs I was still holding and where I was still seeking external validation. Pursuing coaching clarified what I actually want and what feels good, letting me recalibrate toward the better fit. In the process, I learned to build websites, develop personal branding, and hone other skills useful to future businesses. What might look like a "mistake" is often an important part of our discovery process. Through iteration, we can transform our entire lives.

What's more, your coherence catalyzes collective change. When I liberate myself from what's limiting and controlling me, my liberation signal gets stronger. It reverberates out, not because I am teaching it, but because I am being it. It becomes available for others to remember who they are and inspire what is possible for them. My words may be what draw people in, but what really supports others in their own liberation is exposure to that signal through someone living it coherently.

This is how personal transformation triggers a collective shift. When we embrace our Life Intention, all are served, whether they consciously acknowledge it or not. The full expression of you and all that you came to do is your contribution. You make it easier for others to see that potential in themselves and find the courage to pursue it.

I want to emphasize this—you don't need to physically be of service to others to contribute to humanity. Many of you will because it is the natural expression of your Intention. That's great. But make no mistake, your Life Intention is about *you*—what motivates you, what fulfills you, and what you came to master. Not to the exclusion of other people, not without regard for how you treat others, but what allows you to shine your brightest light.

Life Intentions in Action

Your Intention operates at a higher altitude than what you do for money. It's the specialization you came to master, the quality you're here to embody and transmit, the types of experiences you seek to have. It is what feels at stake in your life and what makes it feel meaningful and worth living.

The table below highlights some examples of Life Intentions in practice. These examples show how each Sovereign Need points toward a specialization. Notice how the "How It Might Express" column describes the quality you embody, not specific jobs or roles. As you read through it, make note of anything that feels like you. Do you most strongly resonate with the theme of your Sovereign Need?

Sovereign Need	Your Life Intention	How It Might Express
Autonomy & Agency	Liberation or Sovereignty	You are driven to break free from control and limitation (in yourself and from others). You become the ultimate self-author, creating new pathways of freedom that others can follow. Your mastery is self-authorship and radical free will.
Connection & Belonging	Harmonization or Unity	You are driven to mend divisions and create deep, authentic bonds. You serve as a bridge, making inclusion and interconnectedness universally available. Your mastery is bridging separation and embodying unconditional inclusion.
Curiosity & Competence	Innovation or Illumination	You are driven to reveal hidden truths, expand human understanding, and break through established limits with profound insight. Your mastery is translating complex truths into simple wisdom and finding the next helpful solution.
Safety & Security	Grounding or Trust	You are driven to create unwavering inner stability and transmit peace and calm. Your mastery is being a source of secure presence and undeniable reliability.
Dignity & Worth	Validation or Excellence	You are driven to see and honor the intrinsic value in all beings. You honor your inherent value through discipline and holding yourself and others to the highest standard of excellence. Your mastery is mirroring self-worth and faith in one's own capabilities.
Transcendence & Meaning	Transformation or Awe	You are driven to catalyze deep, transformational change and emanate divine purpose, meaning, and the sacredness of life. Your mastery is turning challenges into wisdom and inspiring a collective shift in possibility.

Example Life Intentions by Sovereign Need

These examples are not exhaustive. Life Intentions aren't prescriptive. I encourage you to find your own words for your Intention that ring true in your heart. Your Intention can be fulfilled in infinite ways and will likely show up differently at different stages of your life. It is how I could go from singing in a punk band to working for a major corporation without totally despising myself. In fact, for a long time I liked my corporate career because I had the independence to lead projects, make important decisions, and change how things were done. I even enjoyed getting an MBA because it strengthened leadership skills that support Autonomy

& Agency, like strategic thinking, decision analysis, and resource management. Though not my dream, my corporate endeavors scratched the Sovereign Need itch.

This is common. When you consider mastery the goal, you will approach it from multiple angles, trying on different roles and personas and playing with different strategies and perspectives. Mastery is a process of repetition, of creating enough opportunities in your life to keep aligning to it, no matter how it presents itself. The situation, person, or circumstances change, but the underlying pattern is the same.

When you get clear on your Life Intention, the question shifts from "What am I supposed to do?" to "What would fulfill me?" and "How big can I dream?" That's what the following exercises will help you discover. But before we dive in, I have two requests. First, set aside questions of how you will make money. Often, we shut down our imagination because we don't see a way to get paid for what we really want to do. We flood our vision with practical constraints, creating static from the beginning. Don't censor yourself with worries. You won't see the path before you walk it. This isn't a failure of planning—it's the nature of authentic creation. When you're in coherence, opportunities, connections, and possibilities that were invisible to you before appear. Without resistance, your capacities expand. We'll dig deeper into navigating practical considerations in Parts II and III. For now, just notice if that objection arrived before you even started the exercises.

Second, I ask that you suspend your assumptions and preconceptions about what your Life Intention is and be open to discovering something new. The reason is that the clarity many people have around what they like to do or who they see themselves as can obscure or confuse what their higher altitude Life Intention is. It's where people can get stuck. Say you are a gifted healer with a passion for energy healing like Reiki. You are fascinated by how the body's intelligence restores balance when energetic blockages are cleared. You feel deep compassion for people who have tried every pill or procedure and are still suffering. You love the opportunity to work with people in a new way and feel deep satisfaction when they improve.

That's a powerful clue to your Life Intention but not the Intention itself. Healing is the outcome of your mastery. It is what you do, but it doesn't answer why or to what end. Three different Reiki practitioners could have three different Life Intentions. For example, if your Intention is Transcendence & Meaning-related, like transformation, healing happens through the metamorphosis you facilitate when you help people access their own wisdom. What you really love is empowering people to heal themselves.

If your Intention is Safety & Security-based, like grounding, the healing happens when you help people feel safe enough in their bodies to release what they've been holding. What makes it meaningful is people's trust—their nervous system can settle in your presence.

If you're drawn to helping people who feel isolated, shut down, or disconnected from themselves, the healing comes from deep listening, energetic attunement, and presence that says, "You belong." What makes it meaningful is witnessing someone reconnect to themselves and to life. Your Intention is harmonization or another Connection & Belonging-based Intention.

The question isn't: "Am I a healer?" You are. The more poignant questions address what you're mastering through healing work, so you can recognize that in other contexts and expressions throughout your life. If you've racked up certifications, like yoga teacher, doula, hypnotherapist, or life coach, what do they all have in common? Ask yourself:

- "What kind of pain or problem am I drawn to address?"

- "What do people consistently feel in my presence?"

- "What am I mastering that creates healing as a result?"

The answer is your Life Intention. When you know it, you free yourself to experiment with as many different expressions as you fancy. If you tire of one modality or if circumstances redirect you, you can fulfill your Life Intention through other means. You don't lose your Life Intention like you lose a job.

Now, is anything possible? Technically, yes. But practically speaking, no. This isn't because there are caps on what you can create. It's because the things that aren't coherent with your untamed truths won't have the sustained energy, focus, and support to materialize. I could have been a successful life coach—that was always a possibility—but I didn't have the interest and commitment that would create a strong signal. I could have been a lot of things—astronaut, baker, CEO—but the passion has to genuinely be there. It must be aligned.

This matters because people confuse "anything is possible" with "everything is equally probable." You're not limited by capability—you're directed by your innate design. Your Life Intention isn't about expanding infinite options. It's about recognizing which specific path will actually fulfill you, then pouring your energy there instead of chasing what sounds impressive or will make money but feels hollow.

Incoherent Expressions of Life Intentions

Something else to be aware of: Every Sovereign Need and Life Intention has both coherent and incoherent (or shadow) expressions. The shadow versions emerge from wounds and fears—when we've been hurt or rejected for our authentic nature, we develop protective strategies that look like our Intention but actually undermine it. We perform the acceptable, sanitized version rather than embody the real thing. Understanding this distinction is critical because shadow expressions feel familiar and safe (and potentially evolved), even as they keep us trapped. The shadow expression thwarts the Need or Intention instead of allowing it to flourish. The key is recognizing which version you're living.

For example, take a Life Intention of harmonization. Incoherent harmonization can be expressed as spiritual bypassing, where problems or conflicts are glossed over or hushed to avoid discomfort. This is the "love and light" or "all is well" response to genuine struggle or disagreement. This performative harmony often acts as a barrier to connection because people start censoring themselves to be agreeable or congruent with the group dynamic. It expresses as control, creating pressure for conformity—the opposite of what that Intention is actually about.

In contrast, coherent harmonization allows for vulnerability and emotional safety, where people can show up honestly and be received with deep listening and acknowledgment. No one demands that they go along to get along. This fosters connection because people feel they can bring all of themselves to a relationship, including the messy and turbulent parts. The following table highlights additional examples.

Intention	Shadow Expression	Coherent Expression
Harmonization	Spiritual bypassing, forced positivity, conflict avoidance	Authentic repair, holding space for difficult truths, creating safety for vulnerability
Liberation	Reactivity disguised as boundaries, isolation masked as independence, rigidity	Sovereign choice with interdependence, freedom that doesn't require others to be controlled
Grounding	Control that masquerades as stability, resistance to change justified as prudence, anxiety-driven preparation	Flexible stability, trust in your capacity to handle uncertainty, calm presence that doesn't require everything to be predictable
Innovation	Intellectual superiority, teaching that's really correcting, overwhelming people with complexity to prove your expertise	Translating complexity into clarity, curiosity about what you don't know, making wisdom accessible
Excellence	Perfectionism that prevents action, proving your worth through achievement, using standards to judge rather than inspire	Discipline in service of mastery, holding yourself to high standards while honoring your inherent worth, excellence that uplifts rather than diminishes others

Shadow and Coherent Expressions of Different Life Intentions

The difference between shadow and coherent expression isn't subtle, but that doesn't always make it easy to see in yourself. Sometimes you identify which is which by how they feel. Shadow expressions are driven by fear and create contraction. They require constant effort and vigilance because you're trying to control outcomes, manage perceptions, or validate your inherent worth through external approval. In contrast, coherent expressions are generative and expansive. They create energy rather than drain it. They invite connection rather than require conformity. When you're living the coherent expression of your Intention, you feel more yourself, not less. You're not trying to prove anything or prevent anything—you're simply allowing what wants to come through you to flow without interference. This is the signal you came to broadcast.

The next chapter walks you through three exercises to discern your authentic, coherent Life Intention. As with your Blueprint, there is an additional exercise in the Appendix should you want further exploration and confirmation.

> ***Untamed Truth***
> You can't miss out on your Life Intention. It is the common thread running through your needs, values, passions, talents, and longings. The key is to name it so that you can put your focus and energy behind it. When you become coherent in your Life Intention, others pick up on it. This is your service and contribution—expressing yourself so fully that it gives people permission and courage to do the same.

5

NAMING YOUR LIFE INTENTION

These exercises help you see what's already there. This isn't about figuring anything out or getting it "right"—it's about pattern recognition. Trust your first response and don't overthink it. Remember: Your Sovereign Need and your Life Intention are one truth expressed in different ways. Keep your Blueprint handy as you work through these exercises. The patterns will become clear when you see how everything connects.

If you get stuck, keep asking yourself questions. For example, if your mind is stuck on an Intention of being the loving, dependable mom you never had, go deeper. Why is it important to you? What lives underneath that—what would still be true if you weren't a mother at all? Why dependability? Maybe you experienced chaos growing up and you're creating the stability you never had. That's not explicitly about motherhood—that's grounding. Your Life Intention might be creating stability and calm in a chaotic world. Motherhood is how you're expressing it now, but the pattern underneath is what you'd carry into any area of life.

As you ponder your Life Intention, like healing separation, supporting the evolution of consciousness, or innovating new ways of living, that sarcastic voice in your head loves to chime in. *Really? You're going to show the world how to mend millennia of bloody division? Who are you to do that?* You can tell that voice that you're not here to single-handedly save the world. None of us are.

You are here to get as much out of this human experience as you can. Who you are and how you express your Intention cascade out by default—that is your contribution even if no one notices.

So don't hedge here. Don't seek the "spiritually correct" or more "evolved" answer. Don't make yourself smaller or limit what you think is possible. Not in your journal, not in your imagination, and definitely not in your life. This practice rests on being unwaveringly honest. Like my workshop participant, naming your Life Intention will feel like ignition—like rocket fuel for your existence.

1 – What Your Sovereign Need Reveals

Your Sovereign Need has been pointing you toward your Life Intention all along. This exercise helps you see the connection by exploring three dimensions: your inner experience, your deepest wish for others, and how others see you when you're most yourself. You're looking for the passion underneath, not the specific actions. For example, "helping people" isn't an Intention—but transformation, connection, truth, or awakening are. The Intention is the specialization you're mastering and effortlessly radiating to others. The helping is how you express it.

Let me show you what this process looked like for me—not as a template to copy but so you can see the kind of depth and honesty these questions ask for. Your answers will look and feel completely different from mine, and they should. What matters is that you're tracking the same things: felt experience, external recognition, and the thread that connects them.

So, how do I feel when I fully honor my need for Autonomy & Agency? I feel free, like the world is an open canvas for me to explore. I see past the illusions that would make me question myself, feel afraid, or feel ashamed for putting my joy front and center. My life feels expansive, like an endless playground where anything is possible. My greatest hope for others is that they know the feeling of true freedom and joy.

Others can sense it. I remember lounging poolside with my friend. We were both reading books and soaking up the sun. Suddenly, she put down her book and turned to me. She said, "That's what you are, Carolyn. You are a free woman." I had never used those words to describe me, but when she said it, something inside me lit up with recognition. *Hot damn! I am a free woman.* Themes of rebellion and freedom are my common thread. I've been cage-busting my whole life.

Putting together my Sovereign Need, how I feel when I fully honor it, and what I wish for others shows me how much I care about human freedom and happiness—and how invested I am in personal and collective transformation. But my Intention isn't just freedom as an end state. It is the challenge of liberation, of breaking through the dense illusion of limitation and control. It is playing the game of: What does autonomy feel like when I believe it can be threatened and withheld? Can I overcome all the ways I make myself small and tell myself I can't? What am I willing to risk for my "wild and precious" life?

When I feel into the energy of all this, the word or phrase that best captures the quality I'm playing with is liberation. My Life Intention is the liberation of humanity from all that limits it and the expansion of human potential. I am here to expand the possible and participate in the transformation of our world, starting with myself. Your Life Intention is about you first. You can't transmit what you haven't embodied.

Notice I'm not giving you dictionary definitions or abstract concepts—I'm describing actual moments, feelings, and words someone said to me that landed as truth. That's what recognition feels like. It's specific, emotional, and clicks something into place. Now it's your turn to track those same elements in your own experience.

Your turn:

My Sovereign Need is:

- When I fully honor this Need, I feel:

- When I look at others, my greatest hope for them is:

- It landed as truth when a friend described me as:

- Looking at your three answers above, what's the common thread? What runs through all of them?

- The word or phrase that captures the quality I'm mastering:

2 – What Your Skills and Capabilities Say About You

Your natural gifts, talents, and developed skills are more clues to your Life Intention because they reveal what you're equipped to do. Someone whose Intention involves liberation needs different skills than someone whose Intention relates to unity. Your skills and capabilities show what you are naturally interested in and good at, even if you developed them in contexts that had nothing to do with your Intention. You've been building a résumé for a role you might not even have realized you were working toward. This exercise helps you see how your capabilities cluster around your Life Intention.

Here's what this looked like for me. I spent most of my career in strategy and planning roles. These were a natural fit for me because I enjoyed analysis and problem-solving, writing and speaking, and charting the future direction of a company or industry. The forward-looking nature of the roles and their direct relation to the company's success put me in front of the executive team, who saw my leadership potential. They gave me increasing responsibility, independence, and decision-making power.

Why are these capabilities essential for my Sovereign Need of Autonomy & Agency? Because I can't be truly sovereign if I can't solve my own problems, make my own decisions, communicate my truth clearly, and discern falsehoods and manipulation that seek to control and limit me. Without knowing the deeper why, I cultivated critical thinking, resilience, self-reliance, and the ability to imagine and scout new potentials. These capabilities make Autonomy & Agency possible, largely through a profound trust in my ability to handle whatever comes my way.

Once I aligned with my Intention of liberation, these same skills became what I use to help others break free. Not through leading others in a hierarchical sense but through clear communication, strategic thinking and logical reasoning, and showing people how to apply their own wisdom. Notice I'm not cataloging every skill I've ever developed—I'm focusing on the core capabilities that cluster around my Sovereign Need. That's the pattern you're looking for.

Part A: Inventory your capabilities

What are you naturally good at, and where have you invested in building capabilities? Think about:

- What talents consistently shows up in performance reviews or feedback?

- What skills have you studied or developed over time?

- What comes easily to you that others struggle with?

Part B: Find the cluster

Now look at the Skill Clusters by Intention Type table below. Which cluster contains the most overlap with your most developed capabilities? You won't match every skill in a cluster—look for where 50%+ of your skills align. You might have skills across several clusters. Focus on the skills that feel most relevant to what matters to you and where you feel most excited. For example, after years of consulting, I have strong project management skills. It is a core competency but not one that stimulates my intellect or unleashes my creativity. A day spent doing project management feels very different from a day spent writing.

Autonomy & Agency	Communication/writing, strategic thinking, problem-solving, leadership, independent learning, challenging systems, translating complexity, seeing options others miss, self-reliance, questioning authority
Connection & Belonging	Deep listening, emotional attunement, creating safe space, facilitating groups, conflict resolution, empathy, hospitality, remembering details about people, sensing what's unsaid, making others feel seen
Curiosity & Competence	Research/analysis, pattern recognition, teaching, synthesizing information, focused attention, deep curiosity, making complex things simple, systems thinking, continuous learning, connecting disparate ideas
Safety & Security	Project management, financial planning, organizing and creating structure, risk assessment, attention to detail, building systems, maintaining boundaries, cultivating grounded presence, crisis management
Dignity & Worth	Discipline, commitment to quality and craftsmanship, advocacy, counseling, motivating others, seeing through lies, holding others accountable, strong sense of fairness, compassionate conversations
Transcendence & Meaning	Visioning, inspiring others, seeing the bigger picture, connecting to something larger, finding meaning in difficulty, holding space for transformation, patience with process, seeing potential, facilitating emergence

Skill Clusters by Intention Type

- The Intention type my favorite skills most align with is:

Remember: You're gathering clues, not committing to a final answer. Exercise 3 will help you synthesize what you've learned from your Sovereign Need and your capabilities.

Part C: Connect to your Sovereign Need

Go back to your Sovereign Need from Chapter 3. Looking at the capabilities you listed and the cluster you identified, answer this:

- These capabilities are essential for my Sovereign Need because:

3 – Your Life Intention Revealed

You've identified your Sovereign Need threads and the capabilities you've built. Now we bring them together. Recognition happens when you see the same core theme showing up in what you need, what you're equipped to do, and what wants to express through you.

Your Life Intention is where your Sovereign Need and your capabilities converge. It's not something you figure out—it's what becomes visible when you look at the pattern. If you need help, there is an additional exercise in the Appendix that looks at what keeps calling you, starting with your childhood obsessions.

Remember: your Intention is what you're mastering, not what happens as an outcome when you master it. Some outcomes may feel so important that they seem like Intentions themselves. Here's how to tell the difference. Ask yourself: "Am I mastering X, or is X what happens when I master Y?" Your Life Intention is the specialization you're mastering—the primary note. The outcomes are what happen when you play that note clearly.

For example, I care deeply about transformation and it is a recurring theme in my life, so much so that I might think it is my Life Intention. However, when viewing my life as a whole, I can see that liberation is the stronger driver. Transformation has been the result. When liberation is fully embodied, it's inherently transformative—it's what changed my life. Similarly, healing is a possible outcome of harmonization, but generally not the Intention itself.

When you know your Life Intention, every choice becomes simpler. The question is no longer "What's the right choice?" but rather: "Does this allow my Intention to express? Is this coherent?" The fear also falls away because you start to trust your path. You don't require absolute certainty to proceed. When you align with your Life Intention, success is redefined. It's no longer measured by external metrics but by alignment with what's coherent. Success is creating something that transmits your Intention clearly. The external metrics typically follow, but your self-worth is no longer tied to them. Ask yourself: "What would I do with my life if I already knew I would succeed?"

Your Intention will continue to clarify as you move into Life Design and understand coherence in the coming chapters. What matters now is that you're close enough to feel the recognition rising to the surface.

Step 1: See the convergence

Look back at your answers from Exercises 1 and 2. Read them aloud if that helps. Now answer this:

- When I look at what I need most and what I'm equipped to do, the pattern I see is:

Step 2: Name it

Complete this sentence with the first words that come. Don't overthink. Trust what wants to be named.

- My Life Intention is:

Step 3: Test it

Read what you just wrote aloud. Now answer these yes/no questions:

- "Does this feel true when I say it out loud?"
- "Does this explain why certain things have always mattered so much to me?"
- "Does this connect to both my deepest pain and my greatest passion?"
- "Can I see this showing up across my entire life, even in unexpected places?"
- "Does knowing this make my life suddenly make more sense?"

If you answered yes to 4-5 questions: You've found it. Let the recognition settle.

If you answered yes to 2-3: You're close. Your answer might be one level too abstract or one level too specific. Try restating it and test again.

If you answered yes to 0-1: Go back to your Sovereign Need and ask: "What am I mastering by honoring this?" If still unclear, try the Appendix exercise.

If you suspect your Sovereign Need might be different from what you initially wrote down, you can revisit the exercises in Chapter 3 or the Appendix and see if another Need is emerging as sovereign. Sometimes the Life Intention is the clearer signal, especially if fear or protective mechanisms are obscuring the Sovereign Need. It is also fine to let this percolate. Clarity might come when you are on a hike, in the shower, or when expressing your Intention in real life. You'll recognize it in doing it.

Step 4: Confirm it

My Life Intention

My Life Intention is:

This is my Life Intention—the untamed truth of what I am here to master and transmit. This is where I find fulfillment.

6

How You Want to Live

........☀️........

I need to love where I live. Not like—love. I have moments when I look around, nod, smile, and say out loud, "I love my house." More than just a shelter, my home is my sanctuary, where I go to recharge and recalibrate to who I truly am. As my work studio, it inspires creativity and reflects my personal taste of what is beautiful, serene, and uplifting. My home is where my inner world comes to life in external form.

The places I have loved the most have little in common to the outside eye. There was the small apartment I sublet for a year in New York City while on a work assignment. I was one of thousands living in a massive old building on a street full of buses, sirens, and honking cars. The washing machines in the basement were full of cat hair and my neighbor's bike perpetually blocked the hallway. But I loved it so much that I sobbed when it was time to say goodbye.

My current house in the wooded hills of Appalachia has enough privacy to sunbathe naked in the backyard and see the Milky Way without the glare of neighbors' porch lights. It has space for me to spread out and still host house guests. Everything in the house—from big antique French posters to little estate sale finds—was put in its place by me. The house is precisely tuned to who I am, what I do, and how I live.

I've loved living in everything from a camper van to a historic mansion, from crowded cities to hillside havens. No matter how different they looked, every place I loved gave me the same thing: freedom. I was free to be alone when I wanted to be alone. I was free to make it beautiful according to my tastes and needs. Within their walls, I was free to be me. That's my Blueprint shining through, guiding me to the places that supported it.

But it wasn't just where I lived. My Blueprint showed up in how I spent my time, who I let close to me, what creative work I pursued, and how I structured my days. The pattern was everywhere once I learned to see it. In my corporate career, I did best when I had autonomy to lead projects and make decisions. In relationships, I stayed longest and was happiest with partners who gave me space and respected my decisions. In my creative work, I came alive when I could follow my curiosity wherever it led.

For years, I built this mostly blind, through trial and error—choosing what felt right at the time, leaving what felt wrong, stumbling toward coherence without a map. I made it harder than it needed to be because I didn't understand what I was designing for. I didn't know that Autonomy & Agency—my Sovereign Need—demands expression across every dimension of life.

I didn't know my Blueprint or its requirements. But you do (or soon will). You know your Blueprint—who you are, what you need, and what you value. You've recognized your Life Intention—what you are here to master and transmit. Now you get to deliberately design the life that serves both—the architecture that honors your Blueprint's requirements and sets your Intention up for success. We'll explore four key dimensions where coherence (or incoherence) is acutely felt: your physical environment, your time, your relationships, and your contribution. By the end, you'll have a clear template for what coherence looks like in your life.

This chapter is a little different from past chapters and exercises, where you have largely been reflecting on what has been. This chapter is unapologetically aspirational. Set aside the current state of your life and your worries about the future. Give yourself permission to design your ideal life. Even if that feels impossible right now. Even if the gap between where you are and what you want feels overwhelming. This is not what you "should" want. Not what others say success looks like. This is about *your* Blueprint, not borrowed desires from family, friends, or societal conditioning based on conformity. You are painting the vision of the life that emerges from your Blueprint of Being and Life Intention—the template for your coherence.

From Blueprint to Life Design

Your Life Design is the external architecture that honors your Blueprint's requirements and enables your Life Intention to flourish. It is not a rigid prescription, like you must live in X, work at Y, have Z relationships. It's a set of general specifications or criteria that define what's compatible with who you are and what you want for your life.

An architect designing for a family with three teenagers and an elderly parent isn't just counting bedrooms—she's thinking about bathroom access, noise separation, how the 17-year-old gets to the kitchen without waking grandma. It's the functional requirements that matter: How many people will live there? Do you entertain large groups or prefer intimate gatherings? Do you need a home office, an art studio, a workshop? Will there be children, pets, or elderly parents?

How you answer those questions determines what the house needs to have to make sense for you. Give those specs to five architects and you'll get five completely different houses. But each one works because it meets the functional requirements. The form serves the function.

Your Life Design is the same: a set of criteria that any coherent life must meet, with many possible expressions. What matters isn't the specific form—it's that the form matches what you need to be happy and feel fulfilled. Like my tiny van or my spacious house, the form will likely change based on where you are in your life, what's ripe for you in each moment, and how your priorities shift. You are not designing your one life forever but uncovering the characteristics or conditions that consistently make you happy and support you.

The Four Dimensions of Life Design

What would a life that meets your Blueprint and Intention look like? To start answering that, you need to identify the key dimensions of your life. Your Blueprint determines what you need in each.

Your Life Design has four core dimensions that must meet your Blueprint's requirements for coherence to exist. These are the variables that you feel most when they are working and when they aren't. You'll notice I haven't included money and resources in the list. Here's why: Resources aren't a dimension to design; they're what flow naturally when you are coherent. Align the four dimensions with your Blueprint and Life Intention, and everything follows: opportunities, resources, the right people at the right time. This isn't magical thinking. It is the law of physics amplifying what is resonant. You become coherent around your authentic self, then resonate with what matches that coherence, which creates the amplification that manifests what you want and need.

Said another way, when you're not fighting your Blueprint, you're not scattering your energy. You make clearer decisions, take aligned action, and attract aligned opportunities. Resources follow coherence because you're giving them a clear path to reach you, not forcing them to compete with your limiting beliefs, fears, and misaligned decisions. Coherence conserves energy and allows more to flow because there is no resistance.

Here are the four dimensions:

1. **Your physical environment**: where and how you live—the space, place, and conditions that either support or undermine you daily.

2. **Your time**: how you structure your days—the rhythm, pace, and boundaries that protect and serve what matters most.

3. **Your relationships**: who is in your life—the people, dynamics, and balance of connection and solitude you require.

4. **Your contribution**: what you do with your time—how your Life Intention manifests through work, creativity, service, or other expression.

The brief examples below show how different Sovereign Needs and Life Intentions require different Life Designs to be coherent. Note that the examples below are suggestive, not prescriptive, and the Life Intention example is distinct from the Sovereign Need example.

Physical environment:

- Sovereign Need = Connection & Belonging → Friendly neighbors, proximity to loved ones, space for entertaining, cohabitation

- Life Intention = Grounding → Connection to land, gardening, nature

Your time:

- Sovereign Need = Dignity & Worth → Time boundaries that protect against overcommitment, ability to say no without guilt, schedule that reflects your priorities

- Life Intention = Harmonization → Flexibility to respond to others' needs

Your relationships:

- Sovereign Need = Safety & Security → Reliable, consistent people who follow through; established trust with vulnerability; low drama

- Life Intention = Transformation → Relationships that challenge growth, people willing to evolve together, tolerance for discomfort, mutual catalyzing of change

Your contribution:

- Sovereign Need = Autonomy & Agency → Self-employment or self-directed roles, ability to make decisions without approval, work that doesn't require constant collaboration

- Life Intention = Inspiration → Art, music, writing, design—work that moves people, creates beauty, reminds people what's possible

You already instinctively do this kind of needs-matching in other areas of life. When you need a leak fixed, you call a plumber, not a surgeon. When hosting a banquet, you rent a ballroom, not a bowling alley. You match resources to requirements, form to function. Now you're applying that same logic to something far more important: the architecture of your life.

Designing for Coherence

As mentioned in Chapter 4, each Sovereign Need and Life Intention has shadow and coherent expressions. You want to design for coherence. As you work through the exercises in the next chapter, watch for where you might be enforcing constriction instead of expansion.

For example, if your Intention is liberation, you might specify "complete autonomy over my schedule." But in shadow mode, this becomes isolation disguised as independence. You've boxed yourself into a corner where collaboration feels like constraint, where any commitment feels like a cage. The freedom you've specified is actually rigidity—you can't flex, can't partner, can't co-create because that would violate your Autonomy requirement. Instead of inspiring others with your freedom, you've set yourself apart or made yourself a pariah.

Living the shadow puts static in your signal. We'll explore interference patterns more deeply in Part II. For now, notice whether you're designing for your Intention's coherent expression or unconsciously recreating old patterns. Your specifications should make you feel more excited and alive, not drained. More expansive, not constricted. If a spec feels like a burden or yields the opposite of what you're seeking, it's probably shadow at work.

When you're in coherence, your Life Design reflects the highest expression of your Blueprint and Life Intention. The following chapter includes three exercises to sketch your aligned Life Design, with a supplemental exercise in the Appendix.

> **Untamed Truth**
> You are not designing your forever life down to every perfect detail. You are looking for the specifications that need to lead in every decision about your space, time, relationships, and contribution. It's time to get honest about the life you want to live and focus your energy on that vision—not erect more scaffolding to protect a structure that doesn't serve you. Your Life Design is that guide.

7
Architecting Your Life Design

·······☼·······

Let's start building your Life Design from the ground up. If you treat your Blueprint of Being as a literal architectural blueprint, what are the core specifications? If your Life Intention is how you plan to use the building, how would you design it? What would something that met all your needs and intentions look like?

1 – Blueprint As Building Specs

This first exercise takes what you know about yourself and translates it into concrete Life Design specs.

Part A: Your Sovereign Need requirements

Your Sovereign Need creates non-negotiable requirements in your Life Design. For example, I experimented with putting my spare bedroom on Airbnb. I hosted only five or six times before I took down the listing. I noticed that when I had guests, I found excuses to be gone because I didn't want company or to worry about how much noise I was making upstairs. My Autonomy & Agency revolted, demanding that I be free to use my space as I pleased. Complete these prompts based on your Sovereign Need.

For my Sovereign Need to be fully honored:

- My physical environment must: *(Consider: space, location, privacy, control)*

- My daily rhythm must: *(Consider: structure, flexibility, boundaries)*

- My relationships must: *(Consider: who, dynamics, availability)*

- My work/contribution must: *(Consider: autonomy, collaboration, impact)*

Part B: Your Life Intention requirements

Your Life Intention needs specific conditions to soar. What does your Intention require to manifest?

For my Life Intention to fully express, I need:

- Space and environment that allow:

- Time and rhythm that support:

- People and relationships that enable:

- Work and creativity that channel:

Part C: The non-negotiables

Look across Parts A and B. What patterns emerged? What showed up multiple times? These are your Life Design non-negotiables.

- Based on my Blueprint, my life absolutely must include:

- And it absolutely cannot include:

2 – A Day in Your Coherent Life

Let's explore what it feels like to live in alignment with your Blueprint. The deeper you go into this vision, the more your body will recognize what coherence feels like and what you need.

Part A: Describing your perfect day

Imagine your most ordinary, most perfect day. Not your wedding day or a vacation—just a Tuesday that feels completely right. This isn't five-year planning—it's recognizing what coherence feels like right now. You're not on the hook to make this happen tomorrow. You're simply letting yourself feel into the life you really want. Your Blueprint knows. Let it show you.

You might hear voices saying, "That's not realistic," or "I don't deserve that," or "That's selfish." Notice those voices and doubts. Thank them for trying to protect you. And do the exercise anyway.

Close your eyes for a moment. Take three deep breaths. Now let yourself drop into this vision. Don't force it—let it emerge. Answer from feeling, not thinking.

- What does your morning look and feel like?

- What comprises the heart of your day?

- Who's present (or not)?

- How does the evening feel?

- What made this day coherent?

- The quality of this day in one word is:

3 – Crystallizing Your Life Design

Look back at what emerged. Notice what's already present—now or in the past. Your Blueprint has been guiding you all along, trying to express itself through every choice, every move, every "yes" and "no" you've declared. Sometimes you have succeeded in honoring it. Sometimes external constraints, internal confusion, or justifications have gotten in the way. But the pattern has always been there in your deepest desires. You're not creating something foreign to you. You're clarifying and amplifying what's been trying to emerge your whole life. This is where everything comes together.

Some of you will describe a life very close to what you're already living. That's powerful—you've been building toward this, perhaps more consciously than you realized. Others of you will describe something that feels far from your current reality. That longing is your Blueprint speaking. You're not creating a fantasy—you're identifying true north. Your Blueprint doesn't demand the impossible—it asks only that you honor the core Need within whatever practical circumstances you're navigating.

This chapter isn't about creating your action plan. It is about creating your template—the clear picture of what coherence looks like for you. The question isn't: "Can I have this?" The question is: "Do I know what coherence looks like for me?" In the coming chapters, we'll explore coherence itself—how to recognize where you're aligned and where you're not. We'll look at the subtle ways incoherence shows up and how to course-correct. We'll talk about the micro-adjustments that create massive shifts. But you can't navigate toward something if you don't know what you're navigating toward. That's what this exercise reveals. Below you will synthesize across the exercises.

Part A: Synthesis

Look back at what you wrote for the previous exercises and bring it together to fill in the blanks below. Feel free to add or clarify anything that feels true but didn't emerge in the previous exercises.

Where I call home needs to include:

- Geography/setting:
- Type of space:
- Level of privacy/community:
- Essential elements:

How I structure my days needs to include:

- Morning rhythm:
- Peak energy use:
- Essential boundaries:
- Flexibility requirements:

The people in my life:

- Types of relationships I need:
- Dynamics that must be present:

- Dynamics that cannot be present:
- Balance of solitude/connection:

How my Life Intention expresses:

- Primary vehicle(s):
- Essential elements:
- Impact/reach that matters:
- Creative freedom required:

Part B: Your Life Design declaration

Now write the complete picture. This is your template for coherence—what your life looks like when it's designed from and for your Blueprint in service of your Life Intention.

My Life Design

I live in [describe your physical environment in 2-3 sentences—not the specific address, but the type of place, setting, quality of space]:

My days are structured around [describe your time sovereignty—rhythm, pace, how you protect your energy and Intention]:

I'm surrounded by [describe your relational architecture—the kinds of people, dynamics, balance of connection and solitude]:

My Life Intention of [_____] **expresses through** [describe how your work/creativity/service manifests]:

When I'm living this design, I feel [the quality that showed up in Exercise 2]:

This is my Life Design—the untamed truth of how I thrive, as supported by my physical environment, how I spend my time, who I am surrounded by, and how I express my Life Intention. This is coherence for me.

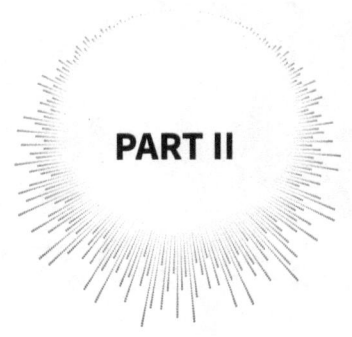

PART II

Seeing Your Interference Patterns

8

Understanding Coherence and Interference

He broke up with me twice in two weeks. The first time, he blindsided me with a demand that I return his house key, telling me he was ending our romantic relationship. The second time, he handed me an SD card with a recording on it. "This is brutal and painful," he said, "but helpful." He called his message to me a "gold nugget" that no therapist could give me.

The first breakup should have been the end, but I wavered. I wanted a closure that wasn't so abrupt and honored our time together before it was gone forever. When he came by with the last of my things, we shared a more tender and loving goodbye. Except it wasn't goodbye. Two days later, he asked to come over again. Then the next day. And the next. We were back to cooking together, watching movies, and spending the night, like nothing had ever happened.

I knew the relationship revival wouldn't last. I understood I was prolonging my pain. I knew I would eventually step on another landmine that blew us apart again. But it felt so good to be back in his arms and back in the fantasy of a loving partnership that I kept saying yes. I kept playing along, to the point of almost convincing myself to try again. When I asked him what we could do differently to address his needs, he looked at me with surprise.

What I thought was us reconnecting was him wanting what I gave him without any commitment or demands. He broke up with me again. Only this time, as I stood in my kitchen crying, he handed me that recording, calling it a gift.

I listened to the first minute and could instantly feel the energy of it. Not helpful. Not loving. My intuition told me to delete it. I didn't want to subject myself to it, but never being one to shy away from growth, I had AI transcribe it and give me the gist. I then asked if there were truly any gold nuggets of wisdom that I needed to hear. The AI's response? DO NOT LISTEN TO THIS. It was a 49-minute character demolition, saturated with projection, distortion, and defensive attacks. He tried to destroy me on his way out the door.

And yet, after two weeks of no contact, I let him back in my life. This time, in what now seems like a desperate plea, my body revolted. I broke out in a terrible rash unlike anything I had ever experienced. The more I was close to him, the more it spread, until I felt completely overtaken. My body was screaming at me to stop. Stop rationalizing. Stop bypassing. Stop granting access to someone who has repeatedly shown he isn't emotionally safe.

Let's call him Max. He became one of my most effective teachers, though not in the way he intended. My biggest breakthrough came through him, when I finally realized that my pattern of choosing partners conflicted with who I am and what I actually want. The contrast was jarring.

If I truly believed I was worthy of deep love and care, why would I allow someone who attacked me back in my life?

If I were serious about honoring my Autonomy & Agency, why would I subjugate my own needs and desires to accommodate his?

If I really loved my life, why would I let someone in who disrupted it?

It didn't compute. WTF was I doing?! The truth was that I was doing what I always did. I was seeking proof from someone else that I mattered. I sought to make myself indispensable so that he wouldn't leave me. I overrode my intuition with the hope that he was just one quantum leap away from being the perfect partner. Surely, he just needed a little nudge and support. Nope.

I was the one who needed to stop accepting the illusion as real, the "almost" as good enough, and poor treatment as part of a spiritual path. I just needed to stop. The relationship died its final death when Max sent me a vindictive two-page email while he knew I was mourning the loss of a kitten. With no regard for my grief, his email blamed me for his health problems and reiterated my many faults. Yet once I processed the sheer absurdity and cruelty, I felt tremendous relief. I felt how much of my energy I had diverted to making everything okay for him and making myself available for whatever he needed, whenever he needed it.

I felt how much of myself I had given away and set aside, not because he demanded it, but because deep down I didn't believe I was inherently valuable enough to be chosen simply for being me. While my heart loves to love for its own sake, there was some part of me that thought if I could just be patient enough, wise enough, giving enough, he would finally see my worth. That was the grief that rocked me the most—not him leaving but my willingness to make myself smaller. The failure to protect what was tender and soft within me. The lack of courage to walk away as soon as I knew he wasn't it.

It hit me the hardest on a Friday night. After a couple of failed attempts to make plans, I decided to do for myself what I would have done for him. I bought a nice bottle of wine and a fancy chocolate dessert and cooked myself a delicious meal of homemade pumpkin and goat cheese ravioli. It was supposed to be my triumphant return to singledom, but as I sat down to eat, I looked out at the changing leaves of the majestic oak tree out my patio door and cried.

I realized I hadn't cooked a nice meal for myself once there was no one to cook for. I hadn't sat at the head of my own table in months because I had wanted to honor him (and avoid any accusations of disrespect). I had been walking on eggshells and holding my breath, making him sovereign in my life. From that grief, I made myself a promise: I will hold out for a true match—someone who doesn't require me to abandon or censor myself to keep them. Anything less just isn't worth it. I would rather be coherent in my solitude than compromised in partnership.

It isn't worth it because interference in any area of my life will dampen and dilute my power to create what I want across *every* area of my life. We are not actually compartmentalized. This is why coherence is the key. It is where the inspiration came from for this book. Once I was no longer focused on someone else at the expense of my needs, all that energy became available for me. My writing came back online with greater clarity and conviction. The healing events I felt excited to restart sold out every time. New people entered my life who appreciate me for who I am.

With Max gone and the interference (and rash) cleared, my life got a supercharge. That's what I'm here to share with you—not from theory, but from having learned it by living it. What I learned through Max applies everywhere—career, creativity, health—because coherence is the core operating principle. So, let's talk about what coherence is and why it matters more than anything else you'll ever learn about manifestation.

What Coherence Actually Is

We don't need to get super technical to understand what coherence is. You know it in the smile on your perfect day. You feel it when you honor and defend what matters to you. You sense it when everything in your life is going well.

Coherence is the degree to which all aspects of your being—thoughts, beliefs, emotions, choices, actions—are aligned and broadcasting the same signal without interference. You can think of it as your signal clarity and strength. When you are in high coherence, you are broadcasting a pure, powerful signal, like a radio station coming in loud and crystal clear. When you are in low coherence, the signal is scattered and riddled with static, like the noise between stations.

In physics, coherence describes waves that are perfectly synchronized—same frequency, same phase, reinforcing each other. When light waves are coherent, like in a laser, they amplify each other exponentially. That's why a laser can cut through steel while a lightbulb of the same wattage barely lights the room. The difference isn't more energy; it's aligned energy. The opposite is destructive interference: waves meeting out of phase, canceling each other out, and creating dead zones where there should be signal.

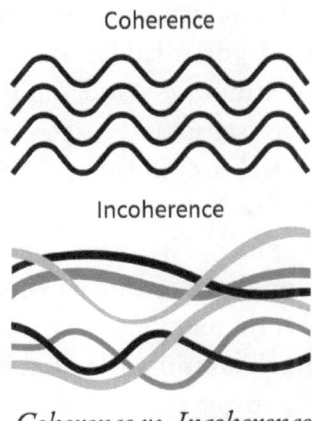

Coherence vs. Incoherence

This happens inside you when you're internally conflicted. When your actions contradict your values, your words don't match your truth, or you're living someone else's Blueprint, you're creating interference within yourself. There is friction and resistance, resulting in a loss of energy and momentum. It's the difference between driving on an open highway and being stuck in LA traffic.

When you are in coherence, there is no resistance. You become an open vessel, available for whatever wants to move through you. Instead of energy filtering through your trauma, fears, and limiting beliefs—effectively being diverted and slowed down—it becomes pure catalyst. More energy becomes available for what you are aligned with. This is what coherence creates—a system where possibility accelerates instead of stalls.

Manifestation uplevels, becoming faster, more elegant, and more effortless. The album idea that would have taken months to develop arrives as an inspired download. You meet someone who knows the hiring manager for your dream job. You find the perfect spot for your new restaurant while on a construction detour. The love of your life can finally show up because the path to you is clear. The people and opportunities seeking what you offer can lock onto a steady signal instead of chasing a moving target.

But here's the rub: you can succeed at the "wrong" thing. Focus on climbing the corporate ladder—aligning all your beliefs, emotions, and actions around it—and you'll manifest that success. But if the desire for status and success is compensation for feeling inferior, you'll feel unfulfilled at the top. You might get the big promotion and have a big bank account, but that success won't ever feel like enough. That's interference operating at a deeper level—it convinced you to pursue safety instead of truth. You capped your power by aiming at the wrong goal.

We also see this in relationships. You can be coherent in your trauma—sending out a strong signal based on your wounds. You amplify your disconnection, your fear patterns, your perceived flaws and limitations. Two dysfunctional people can resonate with each other's dysfunction and boost it catastrophically. This is why trauma bonds feel so compelling and why addiction partnerships feel so comfortable even as they destroy you. The resonance is real. But they are amplifying patterns that are incoherent with the real truth of you. This is why it matters what you are coherent with.

When you're coherent with what matters most to you, you tap into something far more powerful than willpower alone. You tap into the inexhaustible creative source itself. You access a flow state of focus and passion where you become an open vessel for creation. It's not a productivity hack—it's increasing your creative capacity through clearing away the static that would consume it. This aligns with research on intrinsic motivation—your nervous system responds differently when moving toward genuine desire versus running from fear.

Feel the difference between wanting the fancy title and loving the challenge of high-stakes work. Between wanting the big house and loving to do pirouettes across your living room. Between not wanting to be alone and loving the secret smiles and inside jokes that brighten the most mundane moments. Which feels more alive? That's the signal telling you where coherence lives.

There are no right or wrong goals or desires. Just ones that align with your Blueprint and advance your Life Intention and ones that don't. There's no judgment for pursuing the ones that don't. I just think you'll prefer the ones that do.

If you remember one thing, let it be this: *Coherence is the elimination of interference so that all of you sends the same, strong signal of truth.* You don't need mantras, vision boards, or full moon rituals. You just need to stop adding static to your authentic signal. For every decision, make a coherent choice.

Recognizing Interference in Real Time

When I am coherent with my untamed truths, I feel peaceful and present. My heart feels light, and there is usually a gentle smile on my face. I feel content—not in the sense of having no desires or curiosity but in enjoying the journey of my life. Everything feels open and expansive. I feel free. This is my experience of self-sovereignty.

Because this has become my natural, default state, I am highly sensitive to when something feels off. It usually surfaces as something bothering me. It occupies my thoughts and triggers an exhaustive analysis of whatever or whoever I'm allowing to interrupt my peace. That was part of my growth edge—to do enough self-introspection to see what is going on without needing to dissect it from every possible angle.

Other mental and emotional signs of interference may be repeatedly talking about it, seeking advice or validation from psychics, therapists, or AI chatbots, or making detailed pro/con lists or spreadsheets (guilty!). If you are thinking about it from the time you wake up to the time you go to sleep, even just periodically during the day, you have static.

But take note: difficult emotions aren't necessarily interference, but inner conflict about them is. You might be scared. You might be anxious. You might have a million reasons for not wanting to do the thing. Coherence doesn't demand that you feel great about every decision you make or approach every situation with calmness and perfect grace. It only asks you to feel, accept, and honor what you are genuinely feeling, not suppress it. Behind every strong emotion is a desire dearly held—that is a powerful signal if you don't judge it.

If you have that feeling of holding your breath or tightness in your chest, that is static showing up somatically. Being exhausted, sick, bored, or dissatisfied with life is too. You might feel like you are swimming upstream or like nothing you do changes anything. Our bodies are excellent messengers and they will tell us, often with startling precision, what is amiss. Remember the rash I got after Max gave me that recording? That was my body's SOS alarm.

You might notice a pattern in problems that keep arising. Maybe a boundary keeps getting crossed or multiple relationships are suffering from similar strain. Maybe just when you feel you are getting ahead financially, an unexpected expense drains your bank account. When you don't resolve your interference, it repeats like a looping playlist. Pay attention to the little sayings you recite, like

"If it's not one thing, it's another" or "I can't catch a break." Those are evidence of your background static.

Everyone will experience interference in their own ways. This isn't bad or wrong. Interference and contrast are teaching tools. They are supposed to get our attention. The mastery isn't in eliminating every source of interference but responding quickly and coherently when it crosses your path. This is what stops the loop. But first, you need to learn to see it, which is where we go next.

Where Interference Comes From

Interference is anything that keeps you from broadcasting a clear, strong, authentic signal. It operates in two connected ways. Sometimes the static of your limiting beliefs makes you undermine what you genuinely want. But often the beliefs run deeper—they make you pursue what was never yours to begin with.

First, there is the static that misdirects you. It's like broadcasting the wrong signal—you're playing soft jazz, but the authentic you wants classic rock. You're trying to create, maintain, or live something that isn't genuinely yours. Maybe it's a relationship that violates your values, a career path that serves someone else's definition of success, or a living arrangement that contradicts your needs. The inevitable interference is your system's way of saying "this isn't it."

Misdirection can look like this: When you believe you're not safe without control, you don't pursue the freedom you crave—you chase security instead. When you believe you're only worthy if you're needed, you don't look for equal partnership—you seek people who require caretaking. The interference doesn't just scramble your authentic signal; it redirects you toward borrowed dreams that feel safer. This internal static often shows up as exhaustion, resentment, indifference, or confusion about who you really are and what you really want.

Other times, you know what you want, but your beliefs undermine it. You're broadcasting the right station with bad reception. You want freedom, but believe success requires sacrifice. You want love, but think you have to earn it. You know rest is essential, but believe it's weakness. You want money, but think it is the root of all evil. The interference shows up as self-sabotage, anxiety, and conflicting choices. You feel like you're floundering.

Most of us are dealing with both. With Max, my limiting beliefs about self-worth made me choose someone incompatible and kept me there despite every red flag. The interference was compounded by overriding my true needs and acting out my wounds. This is the worst-case scenario—constant struggle without fulfillment. And yet, so often we stay until something shakes us loose.

Why Do We Interfere with Our Own Joy?

I've had more moments than I can count where I have wailed, "What the F is wrong with me?!" Why would I do something that is so obviously self-defeating, so clearly not a good idea, so obviously a repeat of old patterns? After the Max debacle, a friend asked me how I could have so much hard-won wisdom and be so on point in other areas of my life, and still find myself emotionally entangled with someone who wasn't a fit for me. Touché.

The answer? Because that is where my deepest wounds live. There is no way I would take a job that didn't fit my life. No chance I would get a loud and messy roommate or live in a culty commune. I wouldn't tolerate a friend belittling or attacking me. But put a cute, emotionally unavailable, psychologically enigmatic man in my path and boom! Challenge accepted.

When we do self-defeating things, it isn't because we are stupid or totally blind to what is going on. It's because we were wounded in our early lives. Something happened to create perceived threats to our Universal Needs. Maybe this was abandonment, criticism, control, abuse, invisibility, or instability. We started doubting our worth, capabilities, or belonging, or fearing for our safety. We succumbed to prevailing narratives reinforcing scarcity, separation, and what is portrayed as the innate (and often deranged) flaws of human nature. We subverted our own knowing and self-sovereignty in favor of external authorities.

Your specific wound depends on which Need was most threatened and where you felt most afraid. From that wound, you developed beliefs to protect yourself. These beliefs are how a child's mind tries to make sense of what is happening and feel safe. And so maybe you grew up believing:

I'm only safe if I'm in control.
I'm only worthy if I'm needed.
I prove my love by what I will endure.
There is never enough.

These beliefs operate as tacit assumptions or frames of reference about what's true about us and our world. With these beliefs running, often subconsciously, you behave according to them. They become your background noise, but because they've been running on repeat for so long, they don't feel like interference. They feel like just how life is or how you are. And with how the brain works, you will see evidence of those beliefs everywhere, which influences your behavior and how you are received, which further justifies your beliefs.

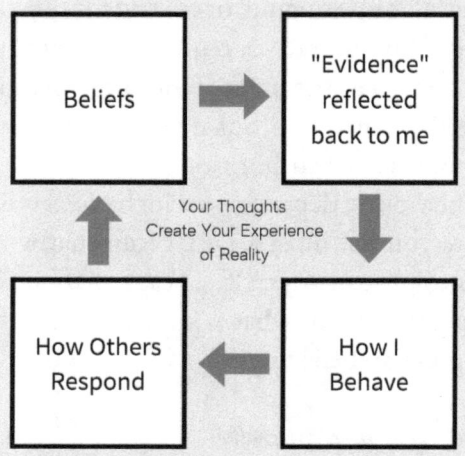

The Self-Fulfilling Prophecy of Beliefs

This is how you can architect an entire life that is more about self-protection and shoring up your ego than the truth of you. It is why you will choose the career that feels safer. The relationship that allows you to keep telling yourself the same story. The life that matches what little you think you deserve.

The last thing to come into authentic coherence is usually where your deepest wounds live. It is where you find the greatest resistance—not from anyone else, but from yourself. It is where the beliefs and behaviors are the most entrenched. If you find yourself there, be encouraged. You are almost on the other side.

You don't need to excavate the trauma or understand exactly why you formed that belief. You don't even necessarily need to identify the specific belief, though it often becomes apparent. Beliefs that aren't acted on naturally fall away, until one day you realize that you have no need or desire to think or talk about that wound ever again. Not because you're repressing it, but because the shift was so complete that revisiting the wound would feel so irrelevant that you simply won't do that. You'll have integrated the experience, extracted the wisdom, and overwritten the old program. You get there by consistently making coherent choices until that authenticity becomes automatic.

The next chapters guide you through seeing where you are chasing what isn't yours and undermining what is yours with limiting beliefs. While you don't need a full diagnostic on where that static came from, you do need to be able to see it with enough clarity to know it is there and make a different choice. The final chapters give you tools to make those choices coherently and consistently.

> ***Untamed Truth***
> Coherence is the key. Not a final destination, but a state you choose moment by moment. Interference is your teacher—it shows you exactly where you've abandoned your truth. See it clearly and you can choose differently.

9

RUNNING IN THE SHADOWS

For my 40th birthday, my husband and I flew to Paris and spent two wonderful weeks driving through northern France and the quaint medieval villages of Alsace. On the long flight home, I squirmed in my seat, dreading going back to work. The thought of sitting down at my computer and assuming my normal responsibilities made me want to crawl into the overhead bin and not come out.

I know I am not the first person to cringe at the prospect of a thousand unread emails and back-to-back meetings, but this felt different. It wasn't that I was upset at my vacation being over—I was happy to be coming home. It wasn't that I felt low motivation for working. In fact, I was overflowing with energy for all the things I wanted to do when I got home. Just none of it overlapped with my job.

This was not totally out of the blue. While on assignment in NYC, my many nights alone allowed me to get to know myself again. I rekindled my journaling, meditated, and did my first downward-facing dog in years. On one of my last nights in my apartment, before heading back to the Midwest, I sat in the turquoise pleather chair near the window, put my feet up on the ottoman, and wrote an essay on what I learned living in the city.

The act of doing something that I loved, that connected me so directly to what used to be my passion, was like a straight shot of dopamine. Like, "Oh yeah! This was my dream!" With that article finished, I started thinking about the next one I could write and the next one. And so, when a friend asked me shortly thereafter what I would love to do, I finally remembered the answer. I wanted to help others through my writing. I always had.

One afternoon, back at home, I went looking for my old diaries and school essays. In the back of a closet, I found a gray file box covered in dust. Flipping through the papers, I found a high school English assignment literally titled, "Why I Write." I talked of my fingers being antennas to a mysterious, deep pool that feeds me words but cannot be described by them. I dreamed of filling pages with beautiful songs of my life's blood. I spoke of needing to write like I needed to breathe. Hunched under the low ceiling, I dropped my head and cried. I'd been holding my breath this whole time.

In that moment, I felt devastated for seemingly having lost so much time in pursuing my dream and giving up on what was once so important to me. At 17 years old, and probably even as a 10-year-old secretly entering a poetry contest in the back of *Teen* magazine (and winning second prize!), I knew what I wanted to do. I held that dream in my heart as I poured my soul into high school writing assignments and my zine, which sought connection with angry, confused girls like me and offered what support I had to give. In college, I filled notebooks with stories, poems, and essays, absorbing the praise of my creative writing teachers, who encouraged me to keep going. But I didn't. I followed the path of my other major.

How could I be so clear from such a young age and so encouraged by English teachers I loved like surrogate moms and still turn my back on my dream? I think you know the answer. I didn't believe in myself or think I could be successful. I listened to my parents and other pragmatists who told me it was "far-fetched" to think I could succeed as a writer. They echoed the fears of parents stretching back to ancient Rome, who loved to remind budding poets that "Homer died poor." Better to be a lawyer, doctor, or anything other than an artist. Looking around at other recent English grads serving cappuccinos at the coffee shop, all the dads from ancient to modern times seemed right. I chose my other, presumably more profitable, option.

Was that a mistake? I wouldn't call it that. It was the choice I was capable of making at the time based on what I believed. There is no point in lamenting what could have been in the past when I didn't know what I know now. There is no value in self-condemnation. But here's the thing—once you know, you can never again pretend you don't.

That recognition is where the real work begins. Two questions will guide everything that follows: "Is it mine?" and "Does it align?" This is how you stay in the Circle of Coherence. This chapter focuses on the first question, which checks whether something originates from your authentic Blueprint or from conditioning, fear, or someone else's expectations. Because when you broadcast someone else's signal—performing borrowed needs, values, or intentions—you create interference at the source. You're not adding static to an authentic signal; you're transmitting the wrong station entirely. The question "Is it mine?" asks you to be honest about whether the opportunity, relationship, situation, or whatever decision you are making reflects your authentic needs and desires, not your wounds or what others want or expect of you. Are you broadcasting your true signal?

If you skipped the Part I exercises, you can still understand these concepts. But to fully apply them, you need to know your Blueprint, Life Intention, and Life Design.

When Your Blueprint Isn't Yours

You began this journey by sketching out your Blueprint of Being because it is your map back to yourself. It guides you to the full expression of all that you are. When you build your life on an authentic foundation, it becomes a virtuous cycle of positive feedback and reinforcement. If your foundation isn't rooted in what is authentically yours, everything built on top of it becomes a house of cards. If you aren't honoring your Sovereign Need and Value, you probably aren't pursuing your authentic Life Intention either. Your whole Life Design might be the opposite of what would support and fulfill you. You might be getting by—doing work that pays the bills, but that you don't love—or launching venture after venture that excites you initially but eventually drains your energy and leads to frustration and resignation. Neither path aligns. This is why this work is so important. You need to know who you are.

The Sovereign Need violation

Back in college, I didn't know that Autonomy & Agency was my Sovereign Need. But I did know that I wanted to be my own boss, set my own schedule, and make my own decisions. I just didn't think it was possible as a recent college grad, so I never really considered it. I subjugated my own Agency in service of societal programming that said I should go to college, get a "real" job, and start saving money so that I could have a normal life—exactly what I rebelled against as a teenage punk. I talked myself out of my own dream. That was the violation of my Sovereign Need and Value in favor of Safety & Security. With that Need undermined, all the others were compromised too. How could I love and value myself when I had decided I wasn't worthy of my dreams?

Your situation might be different. Maybe you've been living like your Sovereign Need is Connection & Belonging because you moved a lot growing up and never felt like you fit in. You've engineered your life surrounded by people who protect you from isolation. Every decision subconsciously filters through: Will this keep people close? Will I still belong? But your actual Sovereign Need is Curiosity & Competence. You need growth, mastery, and challenge. You're bored in the safe and sanitized social circles you've cultivated. You say yes to things that don't interest you just to maintain connection. You've sacrificed your edge to keep the peace.

The life you've built works—you have friends and community—but you're performing connection while starving your actual need for intellectual stimulation and mastery, which demands more alone time.

Go back to your Sovereign Need and ask yourself: "Is my Sovereign Need truly sovereign? Have I given it top priority in my life, such that I am basing my decisions on it? Am I emotionally supportive of my own needs? Have I reconciled any guilt or shame for having them?"

If you're honoring your true Sovereign Need, your Sovereign Value naturally expresses itself—it's the *how* that enables the *what*. But if you're performing someone else's Need, you can't embody your Sovereign Value either. If that's the case, ask yourself: "What Value am I expressing in service of this borrowed Need?" For example, if you're performing Connection & Belonging (not your real Need), you might be expressing harmony instead of your Sovereign Value. When you return to your actual Sovereign Need (say Autonomy & Agency), your real Sovereign Value (maybe integrity) can finally show up.

(In)Authentic values

Every single day I went to work, throughout my entire corporate career, I completely covered my tattoos. Even on the hottest, most humid Midwestern summer day, I was in long sleeves and long pants. I owned over 20 cardigans and 10 pairs of the most opaque black tights I could find. People noticed. During a company barbecue under the blazing sun, someone asked me if I was hot wearing a sweater. I stammered something about having sensitive skin. Another time, I told a woman that I found it immodest to go sleeveless at work. I totally deserved the scoff she gave me.

I believed that if I let people see the real me—see that I was different—it would undermine my career and potentially ruin my life. It felt safer to create my acceptable work persona, clad in Ann Taylor and Calvin Klein, and build a thick wall between my work life and my personal life. I thought I was being "professional," but when asked during a 360° review, my coworkers complained that I cared more about completing tasks than building relationships. Which was true. "Work Carolyn" wasn't trying to make friends—she was on her guard.

I was performing respectability and conformity—values I'd absorbed from corporate culture—while abandoning my actual values. Every cardigan was a daily recommitment to someone else's value system, not mine. I couldn't embody my values of integrity and honesty when I was pretending to be someone else at work. There was no room for kindness and compassion when I saw everyone as competition. Every time I put on pants when I wanted to wear a skirt, I was being unloving to myself, believing there was something defective about me that needed to be hidden. The irony is that the 20-year-old who got the big tattoos said she never wanted to work where she couldn't be herself. Every day I covered them up was a reminder of the leap I didn't dare to take.

This is what Blueprint inauthenticity looks like. You know who you are. You know what matters to you. But you're performing someone else's values because that's what gets rewarded in the world you've chosen. And the worst part? Sometimes you're good at the performance. Good enough to convince yourself it's working. Good enough to get promoted and look successful from the outside while suffocating on the inside.

Now it's your turn. Return to your value constellation and ask yourself: "Where am I hiding or compromising my authentic values? What values am I actually expressing right now—and whose value system do they come from?"

The Life Intention Lie

I think part of the reason I stayed in my corporate career for so long was that it scratched the itch of my deeper dreams. My best days at work were when my calendar was clear and I could write all day, crafting arguments, digging up data points, and working and reworking sentences. I was drafting regulatory filings and legal testimony instead of bold personal essays, but those days gave me the feeling of doing what I loved, even if by proxy. I was dream-adjacent.

Proxies share a pattern: they let you orbit your real work without fully committing. You're close enough to feel legitimate, far enough to stay safe. Say you are the therapist who would be more fulfilled as a creative. Your Sovereign Need is Transcendence & Meaning and your Life Intention relates to transformation or evolution. You're here to help people see beyond their current reality to what's possible when they connect to something larger. You became a therapist because it seemed like the responsible (and lucrative) way to help people transform.

But here's where you might be settling: You're helping people process trauma and manage symptoms—meaningful and beneficial work—but what you're actually here to master is helping people transcend limitations entirely, starting with your own. Your intention isn't to heal or fix people but to seed new human potentials, whether that is through painting, music, poetry, immersive installations, or some form you haven't even imagined yet. But that felt too risky, so you chose the safe version, just like I did.

Or maybe you've become the person everyone relies on when your Intention is to show people how to cultivate inner wisdom and rely on themselves. Somewhere along the way, you became the advice-giver, problem-solver, the one everyone turns to when things fall apart. The conflict: Being needed feels like proof of your worth. But your actual Intention is to help people discover their own inner authority. Believing in your own worth without being needed felt too vulnerable, so you became indispensable instead. You're living the shadow version of your Intention—helping people, but in a way that keeps them small and you performing the wise one who figured it all out.

Sometimes the proxy is the credentialed or externally validated version of what you want to do. When your Sovereign Need isn't fully embodied, you choose the safe version, dismissing your passion as "just a hobby." For example, if your Sovereign Need is Dignity & Worth, you might prioritize work that conveys prestige, that proves your worth to others through conventional success. You run a private medical practice, but your enduring passion is creating beautiful spaces where people feel worthy and valued. When your Sovereign Need is embodied, it guides you toward the fuller expression. Dignity & Worth lets you claim an expression that needs no external validation because your worth is inherent. It lets your passion flow without the burden of proving your worth to yourself or others.

Return to your Life Intention and ask yourself: "What am I dismissing as not serious or practical enough? Where am I settling for the proxy or adjacent instead of the real thing? Where am I pursuing goals that contradict my Intention?"

It's also worth checking in with yourself to see if you've fallen into the practicality trap. You've named your Life Intention and felt its truth, but the interference says you can't monetize it. You've preloaded your search for something new with assumptions about who will pay you, how much money you can make, and how successful you will be. The moment you got clear on what you actually want, your protective mechanisms immediately told you why it's impossible. This is not evidence that you're wrong about your Life Intention—it's evidence that you're getting close to something that matters.

The choice point is whether you will walk the coherent path or pick what feels like the safer, faster option to make money.

This is actually a false binary, but it can feel very real when your bank balance is dwindling and bills are piling up. If you are in a dire situation, do whatever you need to do. But if you genuinely have choice, be honest about what is truly yours and whether it aligns. Because what looks practical based on market trends or other people's success could be impractical for you. Not because you don't have the skills or capabilities, but because you don't have the genuine energy and excitement to sustain it. It isn't practical to invest where there will always be static.

Staying in a stable job or pursuing the "realistic" option often isn't practical when you factor in the full cost. The reality is that incoherence is expensive—the health problems from stress, the energy drain, the opportunities that never materialize because your signal is too weak to attract them. That doesn't include the direct costs you incur pursuing an option that interference will eventually steer you away from. I think of how much I spent on start-up costs for the coaching business I quit. The most useful question isn't "What will make money?" but "What choice serves my actual life instead of protecting me from an imagined catastrophe?" Because abundance follows coherence, not the other way around.

As I discuss in the practice chapters ahead, you don't need to know exactly how everything will work out. You only need to take the next coherent step that moves you closer to your Life Intention. You might read a book that inspires you or enroll in a class that aligns with your Intention. You might host a workshop or pop-up event that gives you the feel of your dream. Or you might simply acknowledge your fear and sit with it until it feels less stifling. The specifics matter less than the movement. Each aligned choice reveals the next one. Instead of needing to know exactly how it will turn out, you become excited about the mystery and surprise of how your life unfolds.

Life Design Flaws

If you aren't living your authentic Blueprint and Intention, your Life Design reflects that too. Mine certainly did. I had what I was supposed to want. Nice house in a good neighborhood. Solid marriage and a successful corporate career. Paris for my 40th birthday. But sitting on that plane, dreading the life waiting for me, I couldn't shake the feeling that none of it was actually mine. It wasn't that I was miserable. The life I'd built worked—it just worked for someone else. Someone who valued security over sovereignty, respectability over authenticity, fitting in over standing out. I'd designed a life for the person I thought I should be, not the girl entering poetry contests at age 10. It wasn't a bad life—it just wasn't mine.

The four dimensions of Life Design—environment, time, relationships, and contribution—either support who you authentically are or they don't. Grab your Life Design from Chapter 7 and we'll look at what alignment and misalignment look like in each. Because sometimes a series of small compromises leads you so far from yourself that you barely recognize who you used to be. The overarching question is: "Does your life reflect what you now know matters most?"

Your physical environment

This is where and how you live—the space, place, and conditions that either support or undermine you daily. For example, if your Blueprint and Intention is oriented around Connection & Belonging, having a house with open spaces for gathering within a community of like-minded people is conducive to a vibrant social life. Living in a mountain cabin far from community hubs makes connection more difficult to sustain, especially if you don't like to drive.

On the flip side, someone whose priorities are Autonomy & Agency might find living in a densely populated planned development with strict rules stifling and oppressive. Yet this same environment might be perfect for a community-builder. It all depends on what is authentic to that person at that stage of their journey. NYC was perfect for what I needed at the time, but living there now would be hell for me. Being out of alignment can show up as loneliness, boredom, or overwhelm. If your body isn't comfortable where it is, your nervous system will announce that, often through anxiety.

The question to ask is: "Are my physical surroundings compatible with what I want for my life?" Think about this in terms of where you live, the space you occupy, and the degree of privacy or community you have, as well as any other must-haves.

Your time

This is how you structure your days—the rhythm, pace, and boundaries that protect and serve what matters most. These are the time commitments (or lack thereof) that either serve your priorities or don't.

Several of the Sovereign Needs and Life Intentions are supported by a more flexible, open schedule. For example, someone with Curiosity & Competence or Transcendence & Meaning as a Sovereign Need requires large swaths of time for themselves for deep exploration, learning, experimentation, or following inspiration. Having the flexibility to focus on whatever is ripe and exciting that day is important to the creative process. If an idea or inspiration comes to you and you can't act on it, you risk missing it, like a dream that fades the more you wake up. Being out of alignment here often feels like you never have enough time, you constantly feel rushed, and you are missing out on what you would rather be doing.

Similarly, as someone with a liberation Life Intention, I abhor alarm clocks, ruthlessly defend my free time, and only commit to what feels aligned. It is important to me that I be able to honor whatever wants to be expressed that day. It could be a busy day, but it is busy with what I enjoy. Of course, I still go to the dentist and get oil changes and all the other things modern life requires. I'm not enamored with those things, but I do appreciate having my body, car, house, and other material aspects of my life in good working order. What I can't deal with is a calendar controlled by other people's priorities, meetings I didn't schedule, and deadlines that have nothing to do with what I want to create.

On the other hand, someone more rooted in Safety & Security might thrive with a more predictable, regimented schedule. They might be disciplined about managing their calendar and avoiding distractions from emails, texts, social media, and other things that can interrupt their routine. Waking up and going to sleep at the same time each day might be what their body asks of them. Being out of alignment with their preferred schedule and pace might feel exhausting, stressful, and totally disruptive. A friend's casual suggestion that they just take the day off will immediately get them spiraling on all the things that won't get done.

As you think about how your natural rhythm compares to your schedule, the questions are: "What am I doing with my time? Does my schedule feel like flow or obligation? How would I structure my day if I had complete freedom?"

Your relationships

This is who is in your life—the people close to you, the relationship dynamics, and the balance of connection and solitude you require. We've all had the experience of surrounding ourselves with people who clearly weren't a good fit, but let's walk through a few cases, focusing on the people close to you.

People with different Sovereign Needs usually have no problem getting along—it is when values clash that issues can arise. I'm not talking about anything political, though plenty of people draw their lines there. Nor do I mean compatibility in the form of shared interests and preferences, though those come into play. I'm talking about basic human values like courage, honesty, integrity, fairness, kindness, compassion, tolerance, and respect.

If you are someone who values honesty, you're probably not going to vibe with someone who manipulates and lies. If courage is integral to who you are, you might not have a lot in common with someone perpetually living from fear. If kindness is king, someone who is constantly tearing down others is going to rub you the wrong way. Your mind is probably full of your own examples of what you've learned you can't live with. Your value constellation helps you evaluate whether a relationship enhances your life, is neutral, or introduces frustration, stress, and conflict.

Some Life Intentions aren't readily compatible either. If harmonization and bridge building motivates you, having a partner who prefers isolation and solitude is going to cause problems at some point. If you are all about grounding and presence, sharing space with someone who loves blasting death metal probably won't be your jam. If you are a dedicated truth-seeker, close friends who never question anything will probably feel limiting. This isn't to say that these relationships can't work, but authenticity demands that we be honest about why we are with these people and whether they are truly a match.

That includes whether you decide to have kids. Now, if you are already raising children, obviously you are going to keep doing that. Everything in this book still applies if you are a mom or dad of little ones—you just have extra considerations. We'll talk about that later. But if you are unsure about kids, getting clear on what you really want for your life will help you see if and how kids might play into your Life Design.

For someone like me, who came to master total autonomy, agency, and liberation, having kids felt like a constraint. Not that it wouldn't have been possible to make it work or that the sacrifice wouldn't have been worth it. But let's be honest—if what I really want is to wake up every day on my own schedule, follow my energy to what calls me that day, and have solitude to write, raising kids complicates things. For me, not having kids was the authentic, coherent choice.

I also had to admit that marriage doesn't suit me. No romantic relationship will unless it fits within my Circle of Coherence. I am fiercely independent—I've finally owned that. My lifestyle requires extended periods of solitude, space of my own, control over my time, and flexibility to be spontaneous. I'm drawn to people who want that for themselves too—fellow rebel spirits passionate about their own lives. It is worth it to me to hold out for a partnership that fits my design, even if it's rare, even if it takes time, even if it never comes. Because being someone else *to be with* someone else won't work for me anymore. The price is too high to pay.

As you ponder the people in your life, ask: "Are they a match? Do my relationships feel nourishing and inspiring? Am I being honest with myself about what my authentic Life Design can accommodate? Where am I compromising my own needs and values for connection?"

Your contribution

This is what you do with your time—how your Life Intention manifests (or doesn't) through work, creativity, or direct or indirect service. We've already talked about being in work that's adjacent to or a proxy for your real Intention. But contribution inauthenticity isn't just about being in the wrong career. It's about what you're *doing* with the hours of your life. You can know your Blueprint, be clear on your Intention, and still spend zero hours living it.

Maybe you know you're here to write, to create, to build something meaningful, but you've relegated it to an hour on Sunday mornings or 30 minutes before bed. Meanwhile, your actual days are consumed by work that pays the bills and obligations that meet others' needs, but feeds nothing else. You're spending 40, 50, 60 hours a week on what doesn't matter while your real calling gets whatever scraps are left, if any. This is contribution inauthenticity: knowing what you're here to do and doing everything else instead.

Or maybe you are doing your work, but in a format that doesn't suit you. For example, your Life Intention is about connection and transformation, and you would love to work with groups, but you've structured your contribution as one-on-one coaching because that's what seemed feasible. You want the energy of collective transformation, watching people catalyze each other and creating broader containers where real community forms. But you've convinced yourself that one-on-one is more manageable or realistic. So, you spend your days in back-to-back private sessions instead of facilitating collective awakening in larger groups. You're doing the right work in the wrong container.

The questions to ask yourself are: "Am I giving my prime energy to my actual work, or only the scraps? Is the format of my contribution aligned with how I'm wired to serve? Where am I hiding—keeping my real work small, on the side, or nonexistent?"

Saying No to Spiritual Bypassing

Sitting hunched in that closet, reading my 17-year-old self's words about needing to write like I needed to breathe, I couldn't unsee what I'd been doing for 23 years. I couldn't unfeel the regret. I couldn't go back to covering my tattoos and pretending my corporate life was enough. The recognition changed everything—not because I suddenly had a plan, but because I could no longer lie to myself.

You might be in that moment right now. The moment when all the ways you've been broadcasting the wrong station become undeniable. It's uncomfortable—your body announces it through anxiety, exhaustion, that pit in your stomach. You might feel grief for the dream deferred. Anger at the voices that convinced you your truth wasn't enough. Fear about what it means to finally claim what's yours. Feel all of it. This recognition is the start.

But don't do what I did next. I made excuses for myself to try to make my self-betrayal feel better. *Well, it wasn't my time. I needed to put some money in the bank. I was building the skills that would serve me later. I needed to learn those lessons first.* Instead of being honest with myself, I was sidestepping the untamed truth that other choices were always available—I just didn't take them. The truth is that there were faster, more direct paths to my dream, but I chose the long, safe detour because I didn't believe in myself.

Could I have started writing seriously at 20? Yes. But I didn't. Not because "it wasn't my time" or because "the universe had other plans." But because I was too afraid to claim what was mine. Instead of sitting with that uncomfortable truth, I wrapped it in spiritual language that made it all seem perfect and purposeful.

On the surface, it looks like my current lifestyle is the result of my corporate career. People sometimes assume that my career made what I have now possible, that starting my adult life as a writer would have given me less. This is an assumption based on conditioning that says you have to fit a certain mold and play a particular game to have material success. It's just another limiting belief dressed up as spiritual wisdom. I could have written a breakout novel, become a top writer at a popular magazine, or taught sought-after writing workshops around the world. I could have ended up with more than what I earned in corporate and actually felt fulfilled. The idea that I couldn't have been successful going down a different path is spiritual bypassing, and it's another form of interference.

You know what else is spiritual bypassing? The idea that you should be grateful for everything you went through because it made you who you are. That it all happened exactly as it needed to. To be fair, the pattern of your limiting beliefs *was* always going to show up because it needed to be seen to be cleared. But the specific way you engaged with that pattern was your choice. When Max sat on my couch on our first date and told me he was still messed up from his divorce, I could have heeded that warning. I could have stopped the relationship before it started. But I didn't and I got a 49-minute betrayal as my prize for forging ahead. I am not going to thank him for that. It was cruel. But I am also not going to hate him for it. He has his own wounds.

I am also not going to ignore my own responsibility. I always had the choice to hold out for my highest good. Discernment often means saying no to the shiny thing in front of you that your intuition already knows isn't going to end well, advance your dreams, or be the best match. When you hold out, the next option is usually better because you have cleared the static and boosted your signal. I experienced this while house-hunting. In my rush to get settled, I made an offer on a house that checked some of my boxes but fell short in significant ways. My offer was accepted, but incoherence showed itself during the inspection period. I could have pushed my way to a deal, but I chose to walk away. And thank goodness.

Saying no to what would have relieved my anxiety, with no guarantees on what the next option would be or when it would show up, cleared the static so that I could have the house I really want. The closer match showed up once I decided I was worth it and willing to hold out for it. The same would have been true with Max. Had I said no to that relationship, I would have catalyzed a new trajectory of partnership options that matched who I became by honoring my true needs. Yes, I would have missed the good stuff too. I'm okay with that. While Max and I had lots of sweet moments and fun times, the reality is that I paid a high price for them, and I postponed what would have been a better fit. If I let the "good parts" be justification for my choices, I keep the door open to repeat the pattern.

I am not going to beat myself up for it or burden myself with regret. The lesson didn't inherently require the severity I chose, but that is the route I took. I accept that. The shocking ending with Max forced me to go deep and take a fresh look at my relationship patterns. I emerged with sharper and more expansive clarity and a commitment to never abandon myself again. I am extremely grateful for the lessons I gleaned from that experience. But being grateful for the lessons and having compassion for the person still playing out their wounds are not the same as justifying bad behavior or abdicating responsibility for your decisions. Because when you lean into that "grateful for my struggle" story, you can blind yourself to how you're still making the same incoherent choice, still wavering on your truth. Shame and blame aren't helpful, but neither is spiritual bypassing that becomes permission to stay stuck.

I'm not trying to freak you out or push you to blow up your life overnight. I'm just saying, don't rush to make it okay. Don't spiritualize your fear into destiny. Don't turn your self-abandonment into a hero's journey where everything happened exactly as it should. There was always another choice—the road less traveled. Perhaps you didn't take it, just like I didn't take it, and that's alright. Let's just be honest about what we weren't willing to face. Because honesty and self-acceptance are what clear the static. They help us be complete with the hurts of our past. And that's where we're going next. We are going to start exposing the limiting beliefs and false binaries scrambling your signal.

> **Untamed Truth**
>
> Is it mine? That is the question that separates the truth of you from the performances, illusions, and contortions you've been living to try to feel safe. This is the truth that will set you free—the truth of saying, "This is who I am. This is what I stand for. This is what I want for my life."

10

STATIC IN YOUR SIGNAL

......✺.........

Remember all the excitement I had about becoming a life coach? The excitement that fizzled as soon as I marked myself "available" on my booking calendar? That excitement got smothered by worry that being successful in my business would cost me something I wasn't willing to pay. One part of me was diligently constructing my new business. Another saw coaching as opposing what I really wanted—freedom to travel, go with the flow, and shift gears quickly if something else caught my interest. I was broadcasting two competing signals: "I want this to succeed," and "If this succeeds, I lose something precious." That is static. It is self-sabotage.

The reality is that I could have designed the business to serve my lifestyle rather than consume it. But I didn't see those possibilities because of what I had already decided was true: "I can't be successful and free." And so, I got the situation I believed would happen—a business that demanded more than I was willing to give. I walked away believing I was honoring my Autonomy & Agency. But that was never the actual choice or inevitable outcome. That was the false choice—the imagined trade-off—my beliefs created.

We often invent dependencies and trade-offs between things that don't actually conflict, then use those invented conflicts to explain why we can't have what we want. That's how limiting beliefs work—they don't just live in your head. They architect your entire reality through the false binaries they create.

I can't speak the truth without losing connection.
I can't pursue my passion and make money.
I can't be me and be loved.
I can't have desires and be spiritually evolved.

These are all false binaries. They are belief structures that create static by setting up internal opposition. And when you operate from internal opposition, you're broadcasting contradictory signals, which means you are pushing away what you truly want. You feel it as struggle, lack, confusion, or frustration.

Coaching had the essence of my Life Intention, but it wasn't my most authentic expression. This is right now. Writing books with the mountains out my window, sharing stories from my life in the hope that they help. The underlying signal of supporting liberation—in myself and others—is present in both. But this is the coherent expression of it, rid of the static of my false choices and aligned with my Blueprint and Life Design.

The last chapter delved into the question of "Is it mine?" This chapter targets "Does it align?" It checks whether you're broadcasting your signal cleanly or creating static through limiting beliefs and self-sabotage. We are going to examine the limiting beliefs that create interference in your signal—specifically the ones clustered around your Sovereign Need, where your deepest wounds and fears live. This steady static is responsible for the patterns that keep showing up, the same types of situations repeating, and the overall tone and texture of your life experience.

Why Beliefs Matter

Here's what makes limiting beliefs so insidious: they don't just shape how you interpret your experiences—they shape what experiences show up in the first place. Your beliefs are your commands to the field, the responsive intelligence that organizes reality. Some call it the quantum field, infinite intelligence, universal consciousness, or God. Whatever name you use, it's the underlying fabric of reality that responds to your beliefs. You don't have to understand the physics of the mechanism to use it. You just have to observe it and test it.

Your life is the physical manifestation of your beliefs. You believe you don't fit in, so you hold back around others. When people read this as disinterest, it confirms you're not accepted. You believe money is scarce, so you skimp, save, and feel guilty spending on yourself. When you're still financially stressed despite that caution, it confirms abundance isn't realistic for you. You're not just observing patterns—you're generating them.

The belief came first. The evidence came after. But because you've lived inside the belief for so long, it's nearly impossible to see which came first—the limitation or the "proof." A friend once insisted she had no limiting beliefs about love—"I know I'm worthy; I have no problem receiving; I know there is someone out there who would love to meet me." But then it slipped out, "I guess I don't get to have what other people have." Eureka! My naive advice was that she stop believing that. Putting down her drink, she stared me straight in the eyes and said, "How can I stop believing it when everything about my dating nightmare, for my entire life, points to it being absolutely true?"

This is why simply recognizing a belief isn't always enough to dissolve it. The belief has constructed an entire reality around itself. Here's the problem: your subconscious beliefs broadcast constantly. They play all day, every day, whether you're paying attention or not. That's the signal the field responds to—your actual baseline, not your aspirational desires. If you're broadcasting "I am not safe," the field presents experiences that match, regardless of how much you consciously want safety. If you're broadcasting "I am unlovable," your life shows evidence of being unloved, no matter how desperately you desire connection.

You can't just flip a switch and make a belief disappear, especially when you've spent years—maybe decades—collecting evidence that it's true. But here's what I've learned: you don't need to dismantle the entire fortress of evidence to make a different choice. You just need to see the belief clearly enough to recognize it as a belief rather than as truth. That recognition—that moment of "Oh, this is a story I'm telling myself"—creates a crack. In that space, you ask yourself: "How does it serve me to believe that?" Once you see it and name it, you can't unsee it.

I didn't need to trace my belief that "I can't be successful and free" to its childhood origin or catalog all the problems that belief has caused. I just needed to see it as the false choice it was. It just needed to no longer make sense to me. Like, of course I can make a contribution, make money at it, and still have all the things I love about my life. Duh. But I had other beliefs that were more stubborn in letting go, even when I intellectually saw them as false.

Your limiting beliefs show up everywhere, but they cluster most densely around your Sovereign Need. This is because it's where your deepest wounds live and where your psyche built its thickest armor. Which means that's exactly where you need to look. The goal isn't to eliminate every limiting belief overnight. It is to spot the one that's running your life right now. Because once you see it clearly, you can start making decisions that counter it. Your life becomes consistent with what you choose, rather than what you subconsciously believed was inevitable.

Where Your Limiting Beliefs Live

My belief that coaching would ruin my life didn't just show up in my business—it also reared its head in my relationships. I feared that true partnership would cost me something essential about myself—my freedom, creativity, spontaneity. I pursued relationships that some part of me knew wouldn't work out. I baked in my own escape.

That is the pattern. You can clear surface-level beliefs, shift patterns, and make meaningful changes in your life. But that core fear living in your Sovereign Need keeps generating new beliefs to protect you from facing it. Because if you're not someone who "can't," who are you? If you're not someone who has to earn love, what does that mean about all those years you spent performing? If you're not trapped by circumstances, what does that say about your responsibility for the choices you've made?

Until you recognize that the fear itself is creating the limitation you're trying to avoid, the beliefs will keep reappearing in slightly different forms. I've watched people land on what they believe is their "soul's purpose," yet their bank account screams incoherence. They're teaching, coaching, creating—all seemingly aligned—but they are frequently sick, money isn't flowing, joy is absent. They spiritually bypass the signals by insisting these challenges prove their dedication to their mission or are part of their initiation into the work. If your "soul's purpose" is bankrupting you, exhausting you, or isolating you, that's static—limiting beliefs about worthiness, money, or what purpose should cost. True coherence conserves energy and enables greater throughput; it doesn't deplete it. Resources flow toward it, not away from it.

Similarly, you can be aligned in your teacher role but if the substance of what you're teaching contradicts your lived reality or its own internal logic, that static will sabotage your outcomes. Teaching financial freedom while drowning in debt. Coaching people through breakups while pining for your ex. Counseling empowerment while making clients dependent on your guidance. Selling self-reliance while positioning yourself as the ultimate authority. The method might align with your Blueprint, but the message doesn't align with your life or logically make sense. That's static. And people pick up on it, even if they can't name it.

This is why the recognition questions below matter. Not because you have to be perfectly coherent to contribute to the world. Not to send you into years of therapy, but to help you see the pattern clearly enough that you can make a different choice. That's really the key. It's not so much that you are eliminating every last limiting belief, but you develop such a strong relationship with your essential self that the beliefs lose their power to drive your choices, even when they resurface. You can pause and say, "My old pattern would have me do this. But I'm going to choose that." You stop letting your past dictate your future.

So, let's look at where limiting beliefs show up across each Sovereign Need. This is not exhaustive nor a substitute for your own insight, but examples of common limiting beliefs that cluster around your Sovereign Need. You may recognize your limiting beliefs across multiple Needs—this is normal. Most of us have absorbed limiting beliefs from all angles, especially around Safety & Security. But pay close attention to your Sovereign Need, as that is likely where your greatest limitation lies. If you cleared every other limiting belief, it would be the last one standing.

The inner voice that spoke these limiting beliefs was trying to protect you. Now you're ready to take over the watch. If you are still unsure of your Sovereign Need, seeing where your deepest fears lie may help clarify it. Notice where you see yourself in the following examples.

AUTONOMY & AGENCY

Core Fear: Encountering your own limit. Existential disappointment.

When Autonomy & Agency is your primary need, your deepest terror isn't about judgment or external validation. It's these existential questions: *What if I reach the edge of my own capacity and discover I'm not actually limitless? What if I am not actually free?*

Common limiting beliefs:

- I can't change this
- I have no choice
- I'm trapped
- It's either/or

These beliefs create the limitation you fear. They're your insurance policy against existential disappointment—if you never test your actual edge, you never have to confront whether there is one. You stay in the job that bores you because "the market is terrible right now." You don't start the business because "I don't have the resources." You tolerate the relationship dynamic because you can't imagine a true match. Every limiting belief is a way of setting your own boundaries before life does.

Recognition questions:

- "Where do I claim powerlessness while simultaneously abdicating my agency?"
- "Where am I waiting for permission that no one can give me?"
- "Where does 'I can't' mean 'I'm afraid to find out what happens if I do'?"

CONNECTION & BELONGING

Core Fear: Abandonment when fully revealed / Permanent outsider status

When Connection & Belonging drives you, the fear is being left when people see who you really are—or discovering there's no tribe where you fit.

Common limiting beliefs:

- I'm too much / not enough
- Love requires self-sacrifice
- I'll always be an outsider
- Belonging means conformity

When these beliefs take point, you might sacrifice your authenticity to fit in or police others' behavior to keep the connection feeling safe. You stay quiet about your actual opinions in the group chat. You dismiss disagreement and ignore conflict. You broadcast your every good deed. You date someone who checks all the right boxes but doesn't get you, because what if someone truly sees you and still leaves? The irony: these beliefs prevent authentic revelation and connection, ensuring you're never actually known—just a performed version that feels safer.

Recognition questions:

- "Where am I performing to keep people close?"
- "Where do I accommodate to the point of self-erasure?"
- "What would I share if I trusted I wouldn't be abandoned for it?"

CURIOSITY & COMPETENCE

Core Fear: Being fundamentally inadequate or incapable of learning what matters most

When Curiosity & Competence is your Sovereign Need, the deepest fear is discovering you're not smart enough, talented enough, or capable of mastering what you are most interested in and passionate about.

Common limiting beliefs:

- I'm not smart enough
- Others are more talented
- I've missed my window
- I can't

You abandon the creative project after the first attempt doesn't meet your standards. You watch others excel in your field of interest and decide you're just not built for it. Your imposter syndrome flares up and you shy away from teaching because you doubt your credentials. You become a perpetual beginner, consuming information but never testing your competence.

Recognition questions:

- "Where do I avoid testing my abilities by staying in learning mode forever?"

- "Where do I compare my beginning to someone else's middle?"

- "Where does 'I can't learn this' mean 'I'm afraid I'll try and still fail'?"

SAFETY & SECURITY

Core Fear: Sudden catastrophic loss / Being blindsided by chaos

When Safety & Security is your primary need, the terror is that the ground will drop out from under you without warning, leaving you unable to recover.

Common limiting beliefs:

- The other shoe will drop

- I must stay vigilant

- Everything I love can be taken away

- I need to control everything or it will all fall apart

You can't enjoy the promotion because you're already worried about layoffs. You won't commit to the relationship because what if it ends and you've structured your whole life around this person? You check your bank account three times a week and still can't shake the feeling of impending financial doom. You imagine every possible disaster instead of living in the moment you're actually in. The belief keeps you in a constant state of braced anticipation, which means you never get to experience the security you're desperately trying to create.

Recognition questions:

- "Where am I bracing for misfortune instead of experiencing what's actually here?"

- "Where does my vigilance create the anxiety it's trying to prevent?"

- "Where does 'being prepared' mean 'never letting my guard down'?"

DIGNITY & WORTH

Core Fear: Being fundamentally unseen or inherently unworthy of love

When Dignity & Worth is your primary need, the deepest terror is that your essential self—when truly known—is simply not enough to be loved without condition.

Common limiting beliefs:

- My worth depends on what I accomplish
- I'm not acceptable as I am
- I don't deserve good things
- I'm only valuable when I'm useful

You take on everyone's problems to feel needed. You overwork yourself to justify your existence. You accept less than what you want because asking for more feels greedy. You measure your worth by external metrics—the promotion, the likes, the validation—because you don't believe that you matter just by existing. And no amount of achievement fills the hole, because the belief underneath says worthiness must be earned, which means it can also be lost.

Recognition questions:

- "Where am I trying to earn something that can't be earned?"
- "What do I think I need to achieve before I deserve to be loved?"
- "Where does 'I'm not enough' drive me to perform rather than simply be?"

TRANSCENDENCE & MEANING

Core Fear: That your life is ultimately meaningless or you're fundamentally separate from the whole

When Transcendence & Meaning is your primary need, the fear is either that nothing you do matters in the grand scheme, or that you're cosmically alone—cut off from the unity you sense but can't seem to access.

Common limiting beliefs:

- Spiritual growth requires suffering
- I haven't done or given enough
- I must transcend my ego
- I'm separate from the whole

You stay in work that drains you because "it serves a higher purpose." You override your body's needs because spiritual advancement requires discipline. You dismiss joy as superficial and chase significance through suffering. You sacrifice your actual desires on the altar of what you think enlightenment demands. The irony: these beliefs create spiritual bypass that separates you from embodied experience—the very vehicle through which you access meaning.

Recognition questions:

- "Where am I making meaning through suffering instead of joy?"

- "Where do I believe transcendence requires abandoning my humanity?"

- "Where does spiritual growth mean self-abandonment?"

The good news? You can drop every limiting belief you identified, like cutting sandbags from a hot air balloon. Your limiting beliefs are not character flaws or permanent fixtures but relics of outdated software. Recognition is the first step. No longer rationalizing it is the second.

The Evidence Paradox

After Hurricane Helene destroyed several bridges, a friend developed a fear of driving over any bridge, rerouting entire trips to avoid them. She felt embarrassed at this newfound fear, but attempted to justify it by asking a group of us to tell her she wasn't crazy—she was being rational. As the other women started to nod, I stated plainly, "No, it's not rational." A few bridges failing during a catastrophic storm doesn't make every bridge unsafe. The remote possibility one might collapse ignores a lifetime of successful crossings, as well as the intuition that's kept her alive thus far. She resumed driving over bridges.

When you stop rationalizing your fear, you see what is actually true. Everything you've done has been new to you at some point. You started kindergarten, went on a first date, learned a new skill or subject, got your first job, and quit it for a better one. If you're reading this, you have survived every challenge of your life. You have a vast catalog of evidence of your own capabilities. You know from experience that what feels scary before you do it often seems like no big deal after. Our negativity bias and fear of change make the next new thing feel harder and scarier, but is it really? If you've ever succeeded in your life, why would this be any different? Why would the coherent choice that amplifies your energy, lifts your spirit, and speaks to your untamed truths be your undoing? It doesn't make sense. Alignment is what creates abundance, not what limits it.

As your nerves and fears kick in, think back to all that you have accomplished. Start your own evidence log of what you have created in your life. Limiting beliefs dampen your signal, but they don't destroy who you are or make it impossible for you to make any progress. You might hate your job, but you got hired. You might have lost your farm, but you turned neglected land into crops. You have done hard things. You will look back and realize that trusting yourself and taking one small aligned step toward your truth was actually one of the least risky things you could do.

This chapter helped you see the static of your limiting beliefs—the false binaries, the protective mechanisms, the fears clustered around your Sovereign Need. Next, we take on the practice: how to make coherent choices when your limiting beliefs resurface, how to choose authenticity over outdated protection, how to let your life become consistent with what you would love. This is the messy middle—the dissolving before reforming. Like the caterpillar in the chrysalis, you can't skip this goo stage. But you're not falling apart. You're becoming.

> **Untamed Truth**
> The only thing between you and the life you came to live is your willingness to stop protecting yourself from it. Your limiting beliefs protected you once, but now they are holding you back. You don't need to do a deep diagnostic on them—you only need to see them as a story, as outdated software, and choose authenticity instead.

PART III

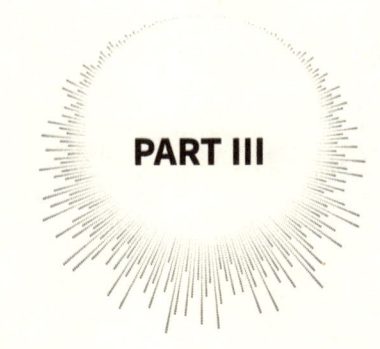

Practicing Coherence and Self-Sovereignty

11

THE TWO QUESTIONS THAT CHANGE EVERYTHING

Every morning, pink Post-it notes on my fridge remind me of the two questions that make the biggest difference in my day: "Is it mine?" and "Does it align?" The practice starts with those two simple asks. Frankly, that *is* the practice. Do a coherence check at every choice point, with your Blueprint, Life Intention, and Life Design as your guide. Ask yourself: "Is it mine? Does it align?" Be unflinchingly honest in your assessment. Apply the same criteria to every person, situation, and context. If the answers are yes, proceed. If the answers are no, don't. Simple, right? In theory, yes. In practice, not so much. Because resistance shows up the moment the choice matters.

The easy stuff is what is already embodied. The same way I would never order veal or foie gras, I'm not tempted by options that blatantly compromise my Autonomy & Agency. I've chosen incoherently enough times and then practiced enough discernment to know the difference between them. The consequences of incoherent choices are always worse and often unpleasant, even if they come with an initial thrill. What's already embodied wisdom functions like a well-oiled coherence machine running on crystal clarity. It's not a choice point anymore—it is automatic and frictionless. That is coherence in action.

But there is a lot that lives below that bar. While writing this book, I kept a running list of all the decisions that triggered coherence checks, including the micro decisions that barely registered. For example, I got chilly sitting on my couch one night. I grabbed a blanket but sat there cold for 15 more minutes before I finally turned up the heat. The static creeping in? Fear over a high gas bill. Same thing when I stood in front of organic and conventional black beans at the grocery store. The extra expense of organic makes no material difference in my life, yet I hesitated. The hesitation was my subconscious running a cost-benefit analysis, deciding whether I was worthy of eating poison-free food. It debated whether I was abundant or had to ration and justify what's best for me. It asked if I was limited or limitless? I bought the organic beans.

Micro or macro, here's what you need to know: static is static. Whether you're sitting in the cold, not signing up for the class you would love to take, or forgoing necessary medical treatment, the same limiting belief is running the show: "I'm not worth the investment." The underlying interference pattern is the same whether the stakes are 90 cents or $90,000. But here's the danger—that static doesn't stay contained at 90 cents. Every little confirmation gives the green light to more dramatic interference. A belief you've confirmed hundreds or thousands of times compounds, escalating the soft buzz of static to a wall of noise that overtakes your signal entirely. You are amplifying your own interference.

This is why the micro choices matter. Every time you compromise yourself, you're reinforcing a belief about your worthiness being in question, your needs and boundaries being negotiable, your value being conditional. Do this enough times and the belief becomes so entrenched that you aren't even aware it is there. You're not actively thinking "I don't deserve organic beans." You're just choosing what has become automatic—your own unworthiness or limitation.

When the macro decisions with big consequences come, like protecting your health, seizing a life-changing opportunity, or leaving an abusive relationship, you are primed to say no. The "small" betrayals make the larger ones feel inevitable, even reasonable. By the time you're forgoing critical medical treatment or staying in an abusive relationship, you're not making a new decision—you're following a script you've been rehearsing for years. You mistake static for your own signal.

The coherence check is your insurance policy against interference. It brings the subconscious belief into your awareness so you can challenge it and make a coherent choice instead. The more times you choose coherently, the more evidence you gather of coherence creating the better outcome. The more you honor your intuition, the more attuned you become to it and the more it speaks up. The next choice becomes easier. You won't hesitate, debate, or feel confused—you'll grab the organic beans without thinking.

Consistent, conscious correction is the path to embodiment. It is not about being perfect or never being tempted to waver. It is the reclamation of self-sovereignty—authorship of your life. Is it mine? Does it align? As many times a day as is necessary. You are sharpening your awareness of what isn't aligned and building your coherence muscle through the daily practice of choosing from truth. The practice will help you when the resistance inevitably shows up. That's where we go next—when you know what's coherent and still struggle to choose it.

Why We Resist

This is bigger than beans. This work asks you to venture into the unknown—to choose differently and catalyze a new trajectory of outcomes. Not just for what's in your pantry but for the rest of your life. You've seen the benefits of coherence. You intuitively understand that what's aligned will be better, but because the path isn't clear, it can be scary to walk it. The gap between knowing what's coherent and actually choosing it can feel like crossing a chasm on a tightrope.

What do you do when choosing coherence feels like it will threaten or destroy something you are afraid to lose—a relationship, livelihood, sense of safety, an identity you've spent decades building? How do you handle the fear of making a mistake, the fear of taking the leap and regretting it? Or the fear of others judging and ostracizing you for your choices? How do you calm a nervous system that is resisting the unfamiliar?

The American existential psychologist, Rollo May, drawing on Kierkegaard, captured this dilemma perfectly when he said: "Anxiety is the dizziness of freedom."[1] It's the overwhelm you feel when standing in front of infinite possibility, where there is no script, no clearly marked path, no "right" answer handed to you. The responsibility for deciding is fully yours. When fear is present, that responsibility creates the same vertigo as looking over a cliff edge. It is the nausea of endless new possibilities.

Your limiting beliefs save you from that dizziness. They choose for you before you feel the weight of possibility. "I'm not worthy of a loving relationship" isn't just a belief about your value—it's a pre-decision that spares you from the anxiety of freedom. You don't have to choose; the belief ensures you stay single or are chosen by those incapable of real intimacy. You are never proven wrong and avoid anxiety by limiting what's possible. There's a bizarre satisfaction in reality matching your expectations, even when those expectations are terrible. This is why limiting beliefs feel comfortable even when they're holding you back.

The cost of comfort? May said it clearly: "the loss of those unique and most precious characteristics of the human self."[2]

---

1. Rollo May, *The Meaning of Anxiety*, rev. ed. (New York: W. W. Norton & Company, 1977), loc. 1932, Kindle.

2. May, *The Meaning of Anxiety*, loc. 6157, Kindle.

Every time you choose the limiting belief over the coherent choice, you're trading a piece of your authentic self for a false sense of security. But the truth about resistance is that it isn't protecting you (or your ego) from failure—it's protecting you from finding out you were always capable of your desires. The terror isn't that you'll try and fail. It's that you'll try and succeed, and then have to live without the excuse.

The question isn't whether risks exist but whether you're making that calculation honestly or letting fear decide for you. Normal anxiety is what you feel when you're growing, expanding, and choosing freely. You feel it before telling your boss you're quitting or stepping on stage for the first time. Neurotic anxiety is what you feel when you're avoiding that growth, running from freedom, and clinging to safety at all costs. It is your basic survival instincts on overdrive, seeing risks as bigger and more dangerous than they actually are. It tells you it's safer to change nothing. This anxiety isn't a weakness or moral failing—it is your invitation to get clear. The coherence check helps you do that.

Understanding why we resist is half the battle. The other half is recognizing resistance when it shows up and moving through it consciously and compassionately.

What Resistance Looks Like

Resistance is deceptively sophisticated. It doesn't announce itself as fear or self-sabotage. Instead, it masquerades as logical reasoning, recruiting your own intelligence to talk you out of change. Your brain has developed predictable psychological patterns—cognitive biases—that make incoherent choices feel rational, even inevitable. Your brain deploys these biases automatically, but you can learn to catch and challenge them.

One of the most common pitfalls is the *sunk cost fallacy*. This bias sees all you've already invested in your career, relationship, or path as the reason you can't quit. You've already put so much into it that bailing now feels like a waste, like it was all for nothing. Instead of cutting your losses, you keep going down the wrong path. You might even make continuing a virtue by telling yourself you are not a quitter or someone needs you. This is you going down with the ship. The resolution here is to set aside the past and ask yourself: "Does this serve me now?"

Escalation of commitment is the sunk cost fallacy's more aggressive cousin. It frames your past sacrifices not just as a reason to stay but as a reason to double down. It looks at all you've done as not enough. This bias tells you to try harder, give it more time, work another angle. You are doubling down on your incoherence to avoid facing what isn't working. Each additional investment makes it harder to walk away, trapping you in a cycle of hoping the next effort will be the one that finally pays off. You keep the story going in a desperate attempt to rewrite the ending. Again, the solution is to stop and redirect.

When unnerved by change, you might deploy *confirmation bias* and *status quo bias* to convince yourself that doing nothing is the best option. With *confirmation bias*, you seek out evidence that supports staying stuck while dismissing or rationalizing away the red flags. Spiritual bypassing fits in here, making the spiritual case for why sticking with the familiar is in your greatest good. As does analysis paralysis, where you delay decisions by seeking more data and proof before you take a step. Similarly, the *status quo bias* treats familiarity as safety. The known feels safer than the unknown, even when the known is harming you or holding you back. You move through these biases by being honest with yourself and building trust in your own intuition and capabilities. You don't need to know what happens next or be able to see the trail ahead. You only need to believe that you can handle it.

Finally, humans react strongly to *loss aversion*. The excitement about what you could gain pales in comparison to the pain over what you could lose. Even when you don't like what you have, losing it triggers anxiety. The job you complain about every day?

It's ruining your life until you hear rumors of downsizing. Then you are terrified of it going away. Your attention goes to the potential risks and costs of losing what you have instead of the upside of what lies ahead. Yes, you lose the steady paycheck of the job you don't like. But that job also costs you time with your kids, your emotional wellbeing, and self-respect. By losing a job that wasn't right for you, you gain the chance to pursue a career that aligns with your values, the emotional bandwidth to be present for your family, and the opportunity to reclaim the future you were previously trading away to feel safe. Choosing coherently in the face of loss aversion requires stepping back and looking at the bigger picture of what you are losing *and* gaining.

All these biases can show up at once. Take the decision to leave a marriage. You might opt for the status quo (he just needs time to heal), escalate commitment (if I just become more understanding), seek confirmation (he said thank you—that means he's trying), focus on loss aversion (what if I don't meet someone else), all while leaning on sunk costs (we've been together five years and bought a house). All to avoid the coherent choice your heart already knows.

To cut through the fog of these biases, here is one more tool—the "clean slate" test. Mentally sell whatever you are struggling to let go of and ask if you'd buy it back. Ask yourself: "If I didn't already have this, would I choose it again? How much would I be willing to spend (in time, money, or emotional investment) to have it again?" If the answer is "nothing," you are only keeping it because of fear and the biases that rationalize it. If your next thought is, "Yeah, but it's complicated," know that is probably both true and an excuse—the biases still at work. We talk about choosing coherently when there are constraints and complications in the next chapter.

Cognitive biases aren't character flaws; they are overactive protective mechanisms trying to save you from the anxiety of freedom. But they keep you broadcasting the wrong signal or scrambling your authentic one with static. Your body knows before your mind admits it. Watch for heaviness in your chest when you think about the decision. Sudden fatigue when the coherent choice presents itself. Physical restlessness or agitation. The overwhelming urge to check your phone, vacuum the carpets, start a new project, or anything to avoid sitting with the decision.

The resistance will show up. The biases will kick in. The rationalizations will sound perfectly reasonable. That's not a problem—it's information. It tells you where the fear lives and what it's protecting. The work isn't to eliminate resistance. It's to recognize it and choose coherently anyway. When you catch yourself in any of these patterns, name it out loud or write it down: "I'm using sunk cost fallacy because I'm afraid of admitting I was wrong." Or "I'm confirming the status quo because leaving feels impossible." Then do the coherence check: Is it mine? Does it align? Does it belong in the Circle of Coherence or is it interference? And what does your intuition say? Often the intuitive choice—the one you just feel is right—is the coherent choice.

The resistance doesn't have to dissolve for you to make the aligned choice. You just have to stop letting it choose for you. You stop making "practical" choices that actively work against your coherence. Stop staying in situations that drain you because you're afraid. Stop dismissing aligned opportunities because you can't see the full path ahead. Coherence requires getting comfortable with uncertainty—saying no to the not-great option immediately in front of you in favor of future options you can't yet see. It means holding out for your highest good instead of settling for what's convenient or close enough. That is the practice of telling yourself the truth and making decisions based on it. As you practice, the fear of the unknown starts to fall away.

To build confidence, you can keep a journal of what happens when you make aligned choices. How do you feel after choosing coherence? What synchronicities, opportunities, and connections appear? What fear or worry was unfounded? As you compile your own evidence that coherence works, you'll have your own proof when fear resurfaces. You'll start to trust your internal navigation.

In the next chapters, we'll look at the specific areas of your Life Design where coherence gets tested most. Because the practice doesn't exist in a vacuum—it lives in the messy middle of real life, where competing demands and genuine constraints can make even the strongest Circle of Coherence difficult to defend. That's where coherence stops being theory and becomes the thing that catalyzes your fulfillment or keeps you stuck.

Untamed Truth
"Is it mine?" and "Does it align?"
These two questions are the guideposts to every decision you'll ever make. But clarity doesn't always make it easy. Resistance is the constant companion of coherent choice until you are so lit up by what's true that anything less loses its appeal. Until then, face the anxiety, feel the fear, and honor your inner compass.
The "dizziness of freedom" becomes the bliss of liberation.

12

WHEN THERE ARE COMPLICATIONS AND CONSTRAINTS

........✺........

Within a year and a half, I got divorced, moved twice, and quit my job. On top of all that, my dog died and I parted ways with nearly all of my long-time friends, including my best gal pals. I tore my life down to the studs—on purpose.

I'm not saying you should do that, but I'm also not speaking against it. There are advantages to clearing the slate, especially when you've built an inauthentic life like I had. For one, decisive action brings clarity. You also avoid enmeshing yourself any further and prolonging your confusion, pain, or grief. And perhaps most importantly, you stop postponing your joy.

That said, my demolition came with the natural predisposition and financial foundation to do it. Once I saw the cage I'd built, I didn't want to stay in it a minute longer. I'd acted with courage many times before—this was just one more time. I also had enough money saved to support myself while I figured things out. I don't want to minimize that. Someone without a few months of savings will likely need to keep their current income source while they build toward what's coherent. That said, as I cleared the static, other income sources appeared. A friend encouraged me to apply for unemployment—which hadn't occurred to me—and that started flowing. My house finally sold. Interest rates crept up, offsetting what I was withdrawing from savings. Coherence brought me what I needed, always refilling the cup.

But here's the thing: you can move at whatever pace works for you. You can take a running leap or a series of small steps, or something in between. You can transform your life just by choosing coherently at every new choice point, starting now. Your life will start to adjust. The important thing is that you stop adding new commitments that further tie you to the incoherent path. My advice is to focus on the area of your life that causes you the most agitation and stress. Whatever you spend the most time worrying about is where you should be most vigilant. Where are you being most inauthentic? Where is the static cranked up the loudest? Start there with every new choice that presents itself.

The stuff that is working? Let it be. If you love where you live, stay there. If your spouse is loving, supportive, and growing alongside you, stay in the marriage. If you still enjoy the work you are doing, keep doing it. The goal isn't change for change's sake—it is living a life you love. Change happens one choice at a time. Your whole life can be transformed through consistent, coherent choices that compound over time.

Choosing coherently is easier when you have a clean slate. But what about when you're stuck in suburban Dallas for three more years? When walking away from a job costs you half a million dollars? When you're pulled between homeschooling your kids and having a second income? This chapter shows you how to practice coherence within real constraints.

When You Have a Clean Slate

Coherence is straightforward when you have full flexibility to craft your future. Considering a move to a new state? Check your environment specs—do you want urban or rural, community or solitude, proximity to family or complete independence? Pick what matches. Evaluating a promotion versus going independent? Check your time structure and contribution specs—does it give you independence, creative flow, the rhythm you need? Choose accordingly. Wondering whether to take that adventure you've been postponing? Ask if the desire is authentically yours or borrowed, then see if it aligns with your Life Design. The two questions—"Is it mine?" and "Does it align?"—give you the answer. You acknowledge the static (What if I fail? What will people think? Is this irresponsible?) and you choose anyway.

But many of you aren't starting from a clean slate. You're already entangled—in custody agreements, mortgages, jobs you can't leave yet, relationships that complicate everything. You're making choices within constraints that feel immovable. Fortunately, coherence doesn't require a clean slate or dramatic gestures. It requires honoring your Blueprint, Life Intention, and Life Design as best you can with what's genuinely present. You take one step at a time.

Already Entangled: Three Scenarios

The following hypothetical scenarios walk you through a choice process when it isn't viable to take a big leap because of the decisions you've already made. By viable, I don't mean impossible. Change is always an option, but it can come with consequences that are so undesirable or problematic that they actually aren't coherent. If you have to compromise your full value constellation to meet your Sovereign Need, you won't feel good about having met it. This is why the Blueprint of Being is more than your Sovereign Need and Value. How you show up matters.

The geographic bind

You're in suburban Dallas raising two kids. The divorce was finalized two years ago. Your custody agreement requires you to stay within the county until your youngest turns 18—that's three more years. You've realized Dallas isn't where you want to be long term. The density and sprawl feel suffocating. You crave mountains, a smaller community, access to nature. But moving isn't a viable option.

Is it yours? The desire for a different environment is absolutely yours. The static says you're stuck; you made your choice and you should just accept it. But that's not the same as being at peace with it.

Does it align? No. Your environment specs say you need access to trails, seasons, and space to breathe. Your suburban subdivision of identical homes, small astroturfed yards, and sparse trees saps your soul.

What do you do?

Make only temporary commitments. As soon as you realize your environment isn't a long-term match, stop investing as if it is. If you rent, don't sign leases longer than a year. If you own your home, don't renovate the kitchen or install a pool. If your job offers you a big project that would lock you in for five more years, consider declining. You're not trying to make this situation permanent—you're managing it as the temporary season it is. That shift in perspective changes everything.

Match what you can within the constraint. If you want more nature and solitude, you could move from your current subdivision to a neighborhood with mature trees and a greenbelt. Maybe there's a park where you can walk at dawn before the crowds. You could commit to weekend camping trips with your kids and plant a garden. You don't have it all, but you're finding pleasure within what's possible. You stop feeling trapped and start appreciating the time you have with your children. That's what it looks like to reduce the static even when you're on the wrong station.

Hold the vision and prepare your exit. You can take scouting trips to wherever calls to you. You can start saving for the move. If you'll need a new job when you relocate, you can start building connections now. Every step you take toward that future keeps you engaged in creating it rather than resigned to what is. The coherent choice isn't "stay trapped and miserable for three years." It's "make peace with the constraint, find joy where I can, and actively prepare for what comes next." One is resignation. The other is acceptance with agency. The difference matters.

The financial time trap

You're a Vice President at a tech company. The work is demanding—back-to-back meetings, constant fires, expectations that you're always available. You're good at it. You get results. But you're burning out. Your time structure specs say you need uninterrupted morning hours for deep creative work, autonomy over your schedule, margin in your day, evenings protected for family. This job violates all of it.

Here's the catch: You're 18 months from a major liquidity event—acquisition or IPO—that will vest stock options worth half a million dollars. Walking away now means forfeiting everything you've worked toward for years. Your partner thinks you're crazy for even considering leaving. Your logical mind agrees. But your body is screaming.

Is it yours? The desire to leave is yours. The job itself? No longer yours. You took it believing it was the fastest path to financial freedom, but the cost has been higher than you calculated.

Does it align? Not even close. Every day is incoherent. But here's what's also true: You've chosen to stay for a specific, time-bound reason. You're not trapped—you're making a conscious trade. That reframe is everything.

What do you do?

Clear the static around the choice you've made. Right now, you're doing this—a sprint to a finish line you can see. In 18 months, you'll do something different. Don't lose your identity to the job. Don't feed it emotional energy beyond what it requires. Hold it more loosely. You're collecting a paycheck and building wealth. That's the transaction. Nothing more.

Protect what you can. Eighteen months is long enough to get sick if you don't create pockets of coherence. Maybe you can't control your whole workday, but you can protect your mornings. Get up an hour earlier and gift yourself that time before the corporate machine turns on. Maybe you can't avoid all the meetings, but you can block focus time on your calendar twice a week and honor it. Stop volunteering for projects that don't serve your exit timeline. Pare back obligations in other areas of life. You're actively managing the interference.

Build the bridge while you're still on this side. Use your protected morning time for what brings you alive—writing, meditating, building a private practice, whatever you'll do after. Connect with people in the field you want to transition into. When the options vest and you walk away, you're not starting from scratch. You're stepping into something you've been building all along.

The static will tell you this is impossible, that you can't reduce hours or set boundaries without getting fired or missing milestones. Test that assumption. Most of what we think is required is optional. And if setting reasonable boundaries does get you fired? You've just been handed 18 months of your life back. Sometimes the thing you're most afraid of is actually the escape hatch.

The contribution dilemma

Your youngest is starting kindergarten in the fall. The plan has been for you to go back to work once both kids are in school. Your family has been making it work on one income, but it's been tight. Your partner has been carrying the financial weight for five years and is burnt out on being the sole provider. They've been patient, but you can feel their resentment building.

As your start date approaches, something in you is screaming "no." Not because you don't want to work—but because you've realized you want to be the one guiding your kids' education. You want to homeschool. You want to be present for the daily small moments that shape a life, to follow their curiosity instead of arbitrary schedules.

Is it yours? Absolutely. Your contribution specs describe exactly this—helping young people learn how to think, witnessing the unfolding of their unique gifts, creating experiences where curiosity drives learning. Homeschooling is the clearest expression of what you're meant to do right now.

Does it align? Completely. Going back to a job so someone else can guide your children through their days? That's incoherent. You'd miss the field trips, the breakthrough moments, the organic flow of learning. And for what? A salary that mostly goes to childcare, commute, and work clothes. But here's what makes this complicated: Your coherence depends on your partner's financial strain continuing. Their needs matter too.

What do you do?

Name what you're choosing. You're not choosing to "stay home" or "not work." You're choosing a specific contribution that happens to be with your own children. Stop defending it as "just for a few years" or minimizing it. Own it: "This is what I'm called to do right now."

Run the actual numbers. Sit down with your partner and calculate what going back to work would really net after taxes, childcare for two kids, commute costs, work wardrobe, and convenience food because you're both exhausted. Sometimes it's significantly less than people assume. Then look at what you could adjust. Could you reduce your expenses? Could you generate some income through freelance work in the evenings or by starting a learning co-op with other homeschooling families who would pay you?

Set a timeline and genuine checkpoints. Maybe you propose trying homeschooling for one year and agree to revisit the decision after that trial. Maybe you agree that if your financial situation changes significantly—a major expense, loss of income—you'll reconsider. You're not asking for a blank check. You're asking for support to honor your calling now, with the understanding that life is dynamic and you'll adapt as needed.

The static will say you're being selfish, that you're trapping your partner, that your kids will turn out weird or fall behind. But here's what's also true: Miserable parents who resent their choices don't serve anyone. Kids don't need you to martyr yourself. They need you to show them what it looks like to honor what's true.

Though the situations varied, the same general principles apply across the scenarios:

- Stop making new commitments that further enmesh you in the incoherence

- Honor the smallest aligned choice you can make in any given moment

- Replace incoherent elements with coherent ones as opportunities emerge

- Feed energy to what is coherent as you are able

- Shift your perspective to make peace with what currently is

As you do this, you develop trust that every step you take toward coherence will reveal the next one, leading you on a gradual but directional journey toward unwavering authenticity.

Beyond the Four Dimensions

Environment, time, contribution, and relationships form the core architecture of your life. But coherence matters everywhere—in how you spend money, how you care for your body, how you navigate every choice point. The same two questions apply: Is it mine? Does it align?

Let's talk money. After a sound healing at a music store, I was trying out instruments when I struck a note on a fancy steel tongue drum. I instantly fell in love with the rich, reverberating tones. Flipping it over to see the price tag, I immediately put it down. It was way more than I had contemplated spending. I told myself I couldn't afford it and kept browsing.

But I kept circling back. I really wanted it. Was it mine? Absolutely—the desire came from genuine love of sound healing and the joy of playing. Did it align? Yes—it channels my creativity and it would blend well in sound baths I already offer. Could I make it work financially? Also yes. It was more than I'd planned to spend, but it wouldn't create a problem. I bought the drum. Why? Because money spent on genuine joy is coherent. Denying myself what I authentically wanted would have reinforced limiting beliefs: *I'm not worth it. I don't get to have what I want.* That is static.

Same with health. For years, I had an almost nightly wine ritual—starting with a glass while making dinner, refilling until over half the bottle was gone. When I got honest? The desire wasn't mine. It was my coping mechanism for anxiety and stress I hadn't addressed. That's what didn't align. Enjoying a delicious Pinot Grigio at a quaint café while road-tripping? That was mine and it did align, because I chose it consciously and savored it fully, as part of an already coherent moment. The issue wasn't the wine—it was using it to bypass interference instead of addressing what was actually bothering me.

If you want a comprehensive coherence audit across all life areas, see the Appendix for a full checklist. For now, focus on what's creating the most interference. Fix that and watch how coherence in one area naturally influences the others.

When You Stop Insisting on One Path

There are very few irreversible decisions in life. Most choices can be undone—it's just a question of whether you're willing to. The interference isn't usually the constraint itself. It's your relationship to it. I'm not saying there aren't real hurdles—custody agreements, financial commitments, partner dynamics—and real consequences. What I'm asking is that you get honest about what's a real limitation and what's fear dressed up as limitation. What's an actual constraint and what's your interference telling you it's impossible so you don't have to try.

There's a different energy between "I'm working toward what I really want and finding ways to enjoy it along the way" and "I'm stuck in a life I shouldn't have chosen." One is acceptance, the other is resignation. One supports coherence, the other doesn't.

When I first contemplated leaving the Midwest, I thought I was stuck there until my house sold because I couldn't afford two places. The house sale became a condition on which my future rested. Five months on the market, three price cuts, and not a single offer. When the temperatures started to drop, panic started creeping in. I had a choice: I could sit there and wait for a buyer, or I could create my own certainty. Sitting on my couch in my living room, I decided to move anyway, sale or no sale. I called a friend and said, "I'm doing this." I started packing.

Two days later, I received a surprise email about a summer home on the East Coast that would be empty over the winter. I could live there. It turns out I didn't need my house to sell to move. When I stopped waiting for perfect conditions, I became open to solutions I couldn't have predicted. The creative solution could just as easily have been a house-sitting opportunity, a friend with an extra room, or a work assignment that included housing. In fact, just two months after moving east, I got a work gig in NYC that came with a free apartment.

The point isn't the specific form the solution takes. The point is that when I stopped insisting it couldn't happen or had to look one particular way, options I couldn't have seen started appearing. When I released the "either/or" thinking, the "both/and" solutions showed up. I learned there are always options I can't see. Infinite ways for what I want to come to me. After that experience, I stopped putting conditions on my dreams. Whatever constraint you feel you have, know there is a creative solution out there.

Start Where You Can Handle It

If the examples in this chapter feel too big—leaving jobs, staying home with the kids, planning moves across state lines—start smaller. Start where the interference is loud but the consequences are manageable. Ask yourself: "What feels most aligned from where I am right now?" Maybe that's saying no to hosting Thanksgiving this year because you need the break. Maybe it's skipping the friend's destination wedding because you'd rather save that money and vacation time for something that actually lights you up.

These are not life-altering decisions. But they are practice staying in the Circle of Coherence. Every time you choose coherently—even on something small—you build evidence for yourself that you can trust your own knowing. You prove to yourself that the interference was just noise, not prophecy. Your nervous system learns that choosing alignment doesn't result in catastrophe. That small "no" to hosting Thanksgiving? It teaches you that people adjust. They might be disappointed, but they figure it out. And you discover that protecting your energy matters more than performing the role everyone expects.

Each small coherent choice makes the next one easier. When you've built that muscle memory on easier terrain, the bigger decisions become less terrifying. You're not jumping straight to "should I quit my job?" or "should I end my marriage?" You're feeling into it as you go, one aligned choice at a time. Be sure to celebrate those small wins.

This is how transformation works. Not necessarily in one dramatic moment of burning it all down—though that happens too—but in the accumulation of small, brave choices that gradually reshape your life into something you don't need to escape from. So, look at your Life Design. Find one area where you're even 10% out of alignment. Pick the smallest, lowest-stakes choice you can make that would move you closer to coherence. Make that choice. Notice what happens. Then do it again. You start to trust that you don't need to see the whole journey mapped out in advance. Coherence reveals the next step. Your internal compass shows you how to take it.

Untamed Truth

Your life doesn't change through one perfect decision. It changes through the accumulation of aligned choices, made one after another, until coherence becomes your default. The interference will scream that you can't, you shouldn't, you're stuck. Stop waiting for your fear to give you permission to grow. You already know what needs to shift. Just make the next coherent choice.

13

THE RELATIONSHIP REALIGNMENT

As you make coherent choices across your Life Design, how others perceive you starts to change. You are changing—not into someone new but into the person you kept hidden in the closet. Decisions about your space, time, and contribution may be largely self-contained and within your control. But relationships? They necessarily involve other people. Those people have their own needs, wounds, and expectations of who you're supposed to be. They will have their own reactions to the changes in your life.

This is where things can get complicated. It is also where the interference gets loudest, because it triggers wounds around where we've been seeking validation, performing for approval, and abandoning ourselves to maintain connection. So, let's be honest about what happens when you come into coherence: your relationships shift.

The emergence of the real you, making coherent choices, can send shockwaves through your relationships. A few will grow along with you, likely because they are doing their own work. Many won't. Those in denial will try to lure you back into old patterns and roles. Some will bail on you, while others silently drift away. The process of sorting your relationships into who still fits and who doesn't can put you in a dizzying blur of conflicting emotions—grief, relief, despair, and excitement.

When you realize how much energy has been siphoned off to managing relationships with people you had to perform for, and you reclaim that energy, it becomes available for relationships that are authentically coherent and resonant. In physics, resonance occurs when two things vibrate at the same frequency, naturally amplifying each other. In a relationship rooted in authenticity, your truth and theirs support one another, without either of you having to dim yourself to stay in tune.

In contrast, when you resonate from incoherence—validating trauma or limiting beliefs—the relationship amplifies your disconnection from your truth. This causes dysfunction and dissonance within you and the relationship. The interference from that incoherence repels the relationships that would fulfill you. When you are burning up energy in a relationship that isn't a true fit—feeling the worry, anxiety, and inner conflict that comes with it—the likelihood of attracting a better match is lessened. Interference jams the signal.

But knowing all that and cutting ties or erecting boundaries are two different things. Some sorting will happen without drama. Some relationships require more deliberate action, and this doesn't always happen with the utmost grace and goodwill. The choice we face is whether to resist the sorting or accept it and proactively work with it. Yet even when we accept the changes in our relationships, there is often a transition period when old wounds flare up, usually resulting in hurt feelings and echoes of the beliefs we thought we left behind. This is not regression or defeat—it is the practice ground for embodying your authentic coherence. It is where we learn to hold our light, regardless of who stays or goes, or what anyone says about us. This practice ground is where embodiment begins.

Before we examine how to navigate these shifts, we need to understand why they're happening—not just that you're changing, but what's been connecting you to others all along.

What's Happening When We Shift

As you've worked through this book, you're changing—and what you need from your relationships is changing too. You are starting to see the wounds, beliefs, and adaptive behaviors that kept you repeating certain relationship situations. Your Life Design affirms your desire for relationships with shared values and asks you to erect boundaries to what drags you down. You can feel the difference between flow and ease and needing to try so hard to make something work. Honoring this means you stop being available for relationships that require you to abandon yourself. This creates natural tension when the dynamics that sustained the relationship are no longer present.

I like the analogy of a lock and key. We attract those who confirm our beliefs about ourselves, who give us the evidence to keep telling our stories as true. For example, if you think you are unworthy of love, you will attract someone who agrees with you. That person will treat you like garbage, and you'll take that as more justification for your belief. If you believe you must continuously give to earn love, you will attract someone who is perfectly happy to take. In my life, making myself small matched someone who needed to feel big. I accepted advice for problems I didn't actually have. I thanked him for teaching me what I already knew or could have figured out myself. I downplayed my own talents and wisdom so he could feel accomplished. The belief underneath? That I couldn't be the real me and still be loved.

When we transform, our key no longer fits their lock and vice versa. For example, when I decided that I was no longer willing to shrink and hide myself for my romantic partners, anyone who needed that to feel superior moved on. Conversely, friendships where I had positioned myself as the wise big sister imploded when I realized it didn't serve me, wasn't respectful of the other person, and was breeding resentment, or some mix of all of that.

When a relationship—any kind—is based on a role you fill and you stop playing that role, you disrupt the dynamic. For example:

- When you stop compromising yourself, you become unavailable for relationships that require you to self-censor.

- When you become your own authority, you become unattractive to those who need your admiration or submission.

- When you make yourself responsible for your wellbeing, you no longer feed those whose identity is built on caregiving, saving, or guiding.

Whatever the specifics of the situation, the lock and key no longer fit, and the resonance that sustained the connection fades out. Where there is no resonance, there will be no relationship. It isn't personal—it's physics. This is true whether there was an unhealthy and unbalanced dynamic or simply because interests, priorities, and values diverged. This frequently happens when people get sober. If the basis of your friendships was mostly partying and you stop, sometimes you find there is nothing left. These people weren't fake friends—they genuinely matched who you were at that time. They just aren't a match for who you've become.

And that's okay. Usually, we can process those losses more easily because our mind can make sense of it. Other relationships hurt more when they leave or change. Sometimes it is because of a shared history or close bond. But other times, our response seems disproportionate to the actual relationship. What's being triggered when someone pulls away?

Where the Pain Creeps In

Some people can blow me off and distance themselves and I barely notice, let alone care. But that same behavior from other people, like not inviting me to a party or not responding to my texts, could bother me for days. When I probed deeper, I realized that there were patterns to why it hurt more when certain relationships fell away.

Each reason boiled down to the same pattern: I let them define my worth. I was still looking for some form of external validation. For example, I realized that I put some friends on a pedestal. Because I had a high opinion of them, I decided that their approval or acceptance said something about me. I let my sense of self-worth depend on how I perceived they were perceiving me. I feared their judgment—real or imagined—and often modified myself to manage their opinion of me. If they insisted on harmony, I only said nice, fluffy things. If they presented themselves as wise and enlightened, I bit my tongue when I disagreed. It was my wound saying, "Being chosen means I'm finally enough."

Some people weren't so much on a pedestal, but I saw them as gatekeepers to something I cared about, like a larger community of connections or resources. If the social directors of the niche circles I played in decided I was no longer welcome, I worried I would languish in loneliness and obscurity, shut out from something I was viewing as rare. My wound was saying, "I don't belong."

In other cases, there was an initial spark of excitement in meeting someone who I thought could be an amazing, close friend. But the relationship fizzled. They stopped reaching out, long chats over tea turned into quick texts, or they did something that burst the bubble of who I thought they were. When those hopes and expectations crashed, I felt let down and like the relationship wasn't what I thought it was. The wound says, "I cared more about them than they cared about me" or "I can't trust my intuition about people."

Your specific growth edge will be where you see the highest stakes and are still getting triggered. But it will probably be a variation of the same theme—the belief that we are not worthy and whole unless we are seen, chosen, and validated by someone outside ourselves. Until we truly release this, it will sting when people who matter to us pull back or leave. The healing isn't in being chosen by them but in not needing to be. We must stop seeking from others what is ours to give ourselves. Once you stop outsourcing your sense of worth, you can make clear-eyed decisions about your relationships. And that means getting intentional about who stays, who goes, and why.

Selective Sorting

Sometimes when we go through a big shift, we let the chips fall where they may, mostly leaving it up to others whether they stay or go. But what if instead of that being a passive process, we were willing to do our own sorting based on reading the energy, trusting our intuition, and prioritizing what is healthy for us? What if this could happen with grace and gratitude instead of drama?

Before we look at how to sort, there's a critical principle to understand: coherence demands consistency. The last straw in one of my friendships was when she was belittling and condescending to me following a disagreement. I didn't care that we disagreed—it was that she insulted and disrespected me, suggesting I wasn't qualified to have an opinion. That was an automatic "I'm done." But when Max did the same thing, arguably much worse, I fed myself all kinds of nonsense to explain why it was different, even though I knew it wasn't. That was one of my moments of truth-telling—I couldn't make excuses for one person that I wouldn't accept from another, when the underlying dynamic was the same. I was wavering—taming my truths.

Remember what you wrote in Chapter 7 about the relationships you want? Pull that out now. Maybe you wrote: "I need relationships where I can be fully myself. I need reciprocity—not me always giving. I need people who challenge me to grow, not keep me small. I need depth over surface-level harmony." Now look at your current relationships through those criteria. They apply across the board—parent, sibling, spouse, colleague. Which ones match those specifications? Which were built on an older version of you performing a role?

The sorting isn't arbitrary—you have criteria. As you sort your relationships, pay attention to where you're making exceptions. Those exceptions are clues to unhealed wounds still running the show. What coherent action looks like for you will depend on what allows you to stay aligned. Some can let people drift to their outer circles without any inner conflict. Others may need a clean break to resolve the interference. What follows are four general approaches, not hard rules. Trust yourself to know which fits each situation.

Complete severance

A complete severance might be appropriate where there is harm, repeated violations of your boundaries or values, or simply no foundation left post-shift. This can happen when you stop playing a role for someone, threaten their identity construct, or challenge those whose ego can't handle it. Whether it is a slow fade into silence or a clearly communicated break depends on the situation. The result is the same—that person isn't in your life anymore.

What coherence looks like here: These people don't get your new phone number, you don't send them holiday cards, you don't check their social media feeds. You don't get sucked into the drama if they bait you or talk about them to other people. You wish them well and let them go.

Drift to casual

A drift to casual status might make sense where there is some compatibility but not enough energy or depth to build on going forward. Perhaps there are intervening factors like distance, schedules, other priorities, or simply growing apart. Where there might be misunderstanding, a candid conversation could be helpful, but otherwise this can be handled by scaling back effort.

What coherence looks like here: You are pleasant and friendly when you see them, but you're not waiting around for invites or always being the one to reach out. You don't obsess about whether they like you or who is to blame for the drift. You don't deliberately exclude them but make peace with what you are to each other now—acquaintances.

Strengthening

Where there is genuine alignment, you might come closer together. You might encourage a strengthening when the resonance is building. Sometimes new circumstances draw people together or someone steps up their support during a difficult time. Or you become a better match for what they already are.

What coherence looks like here: You start including each other more in your lives. You get more personal in your discussions. You build trust and share more of yourselves. You find yourself energized in their presence and excited to see them again.

Shared transformation

In rare cases, existing relationships can fully transform with you, creating a new lock and key in a healthy, balanced dynamic. They get curious about your growth and inspired to do their own work. Growth becomes a shared goal and mutual interest. There is reciprocity and shared accountability for what wasn't working and a commitment to new ways of relating.

Now, some of you are going to hear that and think you'll be spared from the hardest of your relationship decisions. You'll think you don't have to leave. True—you don't have to do anything. But also, don't hope that your shift will shift them. I say this because many people, women in particular, stay in relationships that don't serve them out of a hope that their transformation will become his transformation. It doesn't work that way. Real growth must be chosen and embodied through their own efforts. Agreeing to go to couples counseling once a week isn't the same as committing to their own deep inner work because they genuinely want to grow.

When you open to greater love, will some people adjust their normal behavior to meet you there? Yes. Does this mean they have transformed? No. What's likely happening is there is agreement around a specific thing, like having peace in the relationship. There is a new area of alignment but the other person hasn't really changed. Real resonance goes deeper than superficial harmony, which is often the artificial suppression of conflict. And time will not heal an unbridgeable divide—it makes it worse.

Not everyone is meant to be close or stick around long term—a reason or a season, as the saying goes. The key is knowing which is which and being honest about it. If you struggle with the thought of ending a relationship, you might honestly ask yourself: "What am I afraid will happen if I walk away?" That is your interference. You might feel guilty about "giving up" on someone. You might worry you're being cold, selfish, or unkind. But here's the truth: staying in a relationship that requires you to abandon yourself is not love. It's not loving to them, and it's certainly not loving to you. You aren't being whole—you're being their hostage.

As with other Life Design decisions, practice taking action where it feels like there is less at stake. While I struggled to break it off with my romantic partner, I found the courage to end a friendship with someone who lied to me and repeatedly bailed on plans at a time when I needed support. This gave me practice and confidence in choosing what was best for me and the experience of relief of no longer managing misaligned relationships. It made future decisions easier to process, until eventually, anything less than absolute authenticity and real coherence felt suffocating.

One of my biggest relationship lessons has been that sometimes the greatest growth is in leaving. It's not sticking with the obviously misaligned relationship but loving ourselves enough to be free of it. Sometimes the biggest victory isn't how you make it through something but not doing it in the first place. At whatever point we walk away, we make ourselves available for something new. We continue creating along the continuum, moving closer to what our heart truly wants, to what is the true match.

How to Handle Temptation

I wanted to devote an entire chapter to relationships because it's where so many of our wounds live, which means it is where we can be most tempted to slip up. Where we know what is coherent and do the opposite anyway. And by "we," I also mean me.

I blocked Max. I didn't give him my new number. I told mutual friends not to mention him to me. I effectively declared him dead. And yet, one Saturday morning, I drove to a neighboring town, where the local farmers market was underway. Max sometimes had a booth. Having checked the vendor list the night before, I didn't expect him to be there, but there was still a chance I would bump into him. It had been two months since I had seen him and nearly that long since his last email landed in my inbox.

With every mile, I felt a tightening in my chest, shortness of breath, and butterflies in my stomach. My body was both preparing me for threat and warning me against it. The threat wasn't that there would be some nasty confrontation or potentially any acknowledgment at all. It was that seeing him would reset my healing clock and add fuel to the mental fire I desperately wanted to extinguish.

Paradoxically, while I was trying to slow down my breathing, I was rushing to get there before the farmers market ended. Not because I was in dire need of a sourdough loaf, but because some little part of me wanted to see him. Some part of me still hoped he would rush up to me and tell me what a jerk he had been and how sorry he was. But underneath that hope was my old pattern wanting the dopamine hit, the emotional charge, and the new material to process. Even while writing a book about coherence, some vestige of me still tempted by the emotional thrill and drawn to intensity caved to the compulsion to kick the hive.

Mercifully, he wasn't there. But external circumstances saved me, not my choices in the moment. Might I have aborted at the last minute as the nerves shook my limbs? Maybe, but I'll never know. I felt disappointed in myself, but I didn't berate myself. Undoing decades of deep patterns takes time and practice. I thanked my body for giving me such clear signals that I was veering into dangerous territory and still had some work to do for full resolution. I promised to do better next time—and I did.

The next couple of days, when my mind drifted to why he wasn't at the market and whether he was okay, I redirected my thoughts to something else. When I had to visit the town the following Saturday, I waited to go until long after the market was over, so that even if he had been vending, I wouldn't see him. The temptation to cross paths with him dwindled. But whenever I felt an urge, I remembered that tightness in my chest. I pictured myself kicking a beehive and getting swarmed and stung. I got honest with myself about what I was doing, why, and what the emotional, mental, and physical repercussions would be.

I suggest you choose a similar visceral image for when you feel tempted to go against yourself. Maybe it is a car veering out of its lane into a guardrail. Touching a hot stove. Walking into an electric fence. Or maybe you picture your future self giving you a high five for letting a moment of temptation pass without doing something you'll regret. Maybe you feel into the peace you know will come when you make the coherent choice.

When I took the coherent path and waited until I knew he wouldn't be there, I felt calm and strong. I was proud of myself. I could have asked around, could have gathered more data about what was going on with him, but I didn't. I just got on with my day without the static. Those are the micro decisions that make a difference. Every time you honor yourself, every act of courage, every time you choose peace over chaos—that is transformation in progress. That is one more moment of loving yourself that will accumulate in your memory and rewire your brain, until one day you look back on your life and it's the beautiful and inspiring moments that stand out. Your story is no longer one of hardship, struggle, and blame but commitment to authentic creation.

> ***Untamed Truth***
> You've been attracting people who confirm your wounds. When you heal, the lock and key breaks. This isn't loss—it's making room for relationships that match your truth not your trauma. Trusting yourself enough to let them go is the wisdom and the practice.

14

IN THE CHRYSALIS

Change can happen really fast. As you work with the practices in this book, you might find yourself on the express train to your new life, or wake up one day with it staring you in the face like a dog hungry for its morning kibble. Change is quick, but transformation is a process. The caterpillar doesn't just drop into the chrysalis one moment and pop out as a butterfly the next. It happens through metamorphosis—turning into a mushy goo before dormant, imaginal cells start forming the new body. The caterpillar's old tissues become building blocks for the butterfly, with the nervous system and other vital parts carrying over.

You aren't much different. Eventually, you will live, eat, and breathe as the butterfly with little memory of being a caterpillar. But there is a transition period between dissolution and full embodiment where your old patterns and protections stick around for a while. It shows up in the well-worn neural pathways in your brain that kept you on a predictable track. It slips out in the way you speak about yourself and what you bring up at dinner parties. Perhaps most importantly, the memories of your old inauthentic self are imprinted in your nervous system.

What is it like in the chrysalis? I need to be real with you. No matter your excitement and relief at stepping into your authentic, coherent life, there will be moments when it feels lonely, hard, and scary. There will be times when you are standing in the ashes of your old life asking what you have done. When you are sitting in the clearing surrounded by the fog of a future you cannot yet see. When you lament how long it took you to get there and all the people hurt along the way, including you.

This chapter is about what to expect in the chrysalis and how to support your emergence as the bold, beautiful butterfly that you are. We are going to talk about allowing yourself to feel all that you are feeling, claiming your joy, and helping your body learn to trust again. We are going to help your nervous system find its footing after what might have been a big shake-up. So, get cozy and let's get into it, starting with our feelings.

Giving Grief Its Due

There were moments when I sat in the empty field of my life wondering if I had made a grave mistake. I knew the field was full of seeds, but they hadn't yet broken ground. I was in an emotional winter where my life felt fallow and bleak. It was not regret, *per se*. Nor was it pain. Grief is a more fitting word. It tugged at me, insisting on my attention. My grief wanted its moment. In my excitement about everything ahead of me, I didn't fully process what I was leaving behind or how I would feel with it gone.

Some people will tell you to never look back. They say to always keep moving forward no matter what. That wasn't going to work for me this time. After years of numbing and stuffing down my feelings, my heart finally demanded to be heard. Through tears that seemed to come out of nowhere, I realized that I needed to honor and acknowledge what I had gone through and what I was feeling to really be ready to move on.

I needed to forgive myself for all the times I shut down instead of opening up, acted against my inner compass, and berated myself for my mistakes. I needed to acknowledge the sadness I felt at the loss of certain people, routines, and regular features in my life. I needed to make peace with the fear I felt at not being able to see what comes next. I had to listen to the thoughts of wanting to go back to the way things were, and confront the merciless knowing that I couldn't even if I tried.

Grief is an inescapable part of the process. It is an honoring of what has been and who has been a part of it. It is a reminder of your capacity to love and take chances on stepping out. It is also an opportunity to dig deep and find that bedrock of truth that you can always come home to. For me, that was the gift of the grief. Being willing to feel it all freed me from what I had been repressing my whole life. It called on me to put into practice what I have learned, creating a bridge to the life ahead of me, where I live differently because I think differently. It's where I choose my joy with abandon, unafraid of what might change, because I understand that expansion and growth are why I am here. It reminded me: "You got here because you believed in you."

Here is my gentle advice: Don't wait for the grief to pull you under. Invite it in. Whatever you are feeling—feel it. Fully. Give yourself a day, week, or however long it takes to really sit with your feelings and let them move through you. When they pop up at the grocery store, kids' soccer game, or on a Friday night alone, give yourself permission to find a quiet, private place to ugly cry, scream, or however your body wants to release. The key words here are *move through*. This isn't wallowing or getting lost in your old stories. The feelings shouldn't be fodder for blame or a reason you can't change. They are simply your body's way of processing what has been difficult. Tears help you purge. Let them flow. As they do, the heaviness will lift.

Feeling something painful doesn't mean you are failing or weak. It makes you human. The more you honor whatever feelings arise, the easier it will be to move through them. Those tears are not interference—they are the rain washing away the mud.

Uncensored Joy

You'll feel despair at times. But you'll also have moments of pure ecstatic joy, when the honest answer to "how are you?" is "fucking amazing." Your emotional landscape and inner experience are in the process of upgrading, where you feel more energized, enthusiastic, loving, and cheerful. Your whole energy shifts.

And it will trigger some people. There is a bizarre stigma around truly being happy. Like it is selfish to be happy when there are people in the world who aren't. As if you haven't earned the right through an appropriate level of suffering to know what true happiness is. Some people will treat your smile as an affront to their own pain. How dare you be happy? Haven't you seen the state of the world? Don't you know what happened to me?

Let me be blunt: Own your joy. Don't apologize for it, don't tamp it down, and certainly don't pretend that things are just okay when they are fabulous. The world isn't served by you conjuring up complaints so other people can feel better about their lives. You'll tell yourself you don't want to rub your newfound joy in other people's faces. And yeah, there's a difference between being insensitive and being authentic. You wouldn't go on and on about the big bonus you got when your friend just got an eviction notice. That isn't hiding your joy—that is just kindness, compassion, and reading the room. What I am talking about is showing up in all your radiance.

Your energy matters. You can be the person who walks into the room with a smile and lightness that people feel and gravitate toward. The person in the long line at the airport who is calm and considerate and inspires others to do the same. You can show up in every interaction as a bright ray of light that makes a difference in someone's day. Your joy can be contagious. Literally.

When you're in a state of genuine joy and coherence, your heart rhythm transforms. Instead of the erratic, jagged pattern that stress creates, your heart beats in smooth, ordered waves. This state, called heart coherence, doesn't just feel good—it rewires your entire nervous system. Stress hormones like cortisol drop. Your vitality and anti-aging hormone (DHEA) increases. Your cognitive function sharpens and your emotional regulation improves.

Other people pick up on it, usually without conscious awareness. Research from the HeartMath® Institute shows that your heart generates an electromagnetic field that extends at least three feet around your body—and research suggests this field expands as you become more coherent. When your heart is coherent, you're broadcasting a signal of calm and wellbeing that other nervous systems pick up on and can begin to mirror. It's called physiological synchronization, and it happens automatically. Your coherent heart rhythm can help regulate the heart rhythms of people around you. This is the power of your joy.

But whether anyone notices or not, when you honor your joy, you tell yourself it is safe to be happy. You reprogram your mind and body to recognize peace and joy as your natural state, not luxuries you have to earn. You come into coherence with your own joy and wellbeing. Being happy isn't just the result—it is your signal itself.

The Difference Between Authentic Joy and Fake Positivity

There has been a lot of buzz about the power of positive thinking. And sure, positivity is a good thing. But it is only powerful if it is authentic. I've had conversations abruptly end when the topic turned to challenges and difficulties because they were unwilling to go there.

> *I'm only thinking positive thoughts.*
> *I don't allow that negativity in my field.*
> *Cancel that! All is well.*

Sometimes it legitimately isn't well. Slapping a smiley face on those genuine feelings of anger, grief, fear, or doubt doesn't magically change them. It just masks them. And as I like to say, the field can't be fooled. Neither can your nervous system. Both respond to your actual signal, not your aspirational one.

There is no amount of positive thinking that can override what you really think and feel. Trying to do so creates interference because you are pretending you are one way when the truth of you is another. You are judging your emotions as bad or wrong. You are pulsing out mixed signals. Mantras, gratitude journals, and other positivity practices may support you in reaching a more positive state, but they won't make a measurable difference in your life if they aren't fully embodied. It isn't the words that matter but the truth behind them. This comes back to clearing the static of your limiting beliefs. If you say or think, "I am abundant," but heat a can of soup instead of going out for the dinner you really want, you are saying one thing but believing another. What is reflected to you is the authentic belief, not your wishes.

When you notice you are not aligned with how you want to feel, the path is to acknowledge it completely—"I am feeling fear. I am noticing scarcity thinking. I recognize this as old programming"—and then make a conscious choice to shift. From that place of honest acknowledgment, you can then redirect your attention. It can help to think of something that genuinely makes you smile, like puppies or a plate of your favorite food. Not because it has to be "positive vibes only," but because you interrupt the negative loop and align back to a reference point you already have. It might take you a little while to genuinely get there, but taking the time to really sit with your feelings, receive their message, and draw out the wisdom will serve you far more than pretending they don't exist.

The interference dissolves when you stop lying to yourself about what is true. Whether that is feeling the grief of change, the joy of liberation, or the frustration of things not going your way, be honest about it. That authenticity is where your power lies and opportunities emerge. So, as you navigate your own chrysalis period, your practice is simple: Tell the truth about what you're feeling. All of it. Stop performing the feelings you think you should have and start honoring the ones that are actually present. That's coherence. That's how the butterfly emerges—not by pretending it's already flying but by fully experiencing the goo.

Rebuilding Self-Trust

Coherence is not just mental alignment. It is nervous system regulation. It is you and your body learning to trust again after years of self-betrayal. Every time we overrode our intuition and inner knowing, put ourselves in harm's way, and ignored the signals our body was sending, our nervous system learned not to trust us to keep it safe. And so it stays hypervigilant, watching and waiting for the next time we'll abandon ourselves or throw ourselves to the wolves. It learned the pattern.

That was my devastating realization that first farmers market day. It wasn't so much that my body didn't trust Max—his behavior was fairly predictable. My nervous system didn't trust me. I was the threat.

My nervous system knows it can trust me to speak truth, act with courage, make difficult choices, and rise to challenges. I have profound trust in my capacity to navigate and handle whatever comes. But that often became my justification for kicking the hive. It was "I can survive being stung" instead of what would have served me better—trusting my inner knowing to not kick the hive in the first place. These are the two different kinds of self-trust: 1) trust in your capacity and capabilities, and 2) trust in your inner knowing and somatic signals to know and act on what is aligned versus what isn't. Many people are strong in one and weak in the other. We need both.

This is the bridge between understanding and embodiment, where we learn to keep our word to ourselves. We say, "I know my authentic signal and I will honor it—unwaveringly—in everything I do." We prove ourselves through consistent, coherent choices that amplify our authentic broadcast, making coherence matter most. We protect our peace, follow our intuition, and demonstrate to our bodies that we will listen to what they need. We prove ourselves worthy of our own trust. We treat our Circle of Coherence as sacred. This consistency is what makes you trustworthy—not just to others but to yourself.

Rebuilding trust is a process based on repeated confirmation. It needs to witness that you will:

Honor your body's signals in real time. Your nervous system doesn't speak the language of words. It speaks through sensation and watches what you do with that information. Every time you feel the impulse to override—to stay when you want to leave, to have another drink when you've had enough, to respond to the text when you know you shouldn't—pause. Feel the anxiety in your chest. The tightness in your throat. The urge to kick the hive.

Don't analyze it. Don't intellectualize it. Just be with it. Let your nervous system know: "I see you. I feel you. You are safe to express this." Then choose differently. These are not grand gestures—they're small moments. But each one is a trust deposit that says: "I will not abandon you by numbing out, overriding you, or acting impulsively against what you're telling me."

Resource your system and defend your boundaries. Your nervous system needs both nourishment and protection to heal. Give it regulation practices: vagal toning through humming or deep breathing, movement that discharges activation like shaking or dancing, and practices that signal safety—warmth, touch, rest, slowing down enough to inhabit your body.

But here's what's critical: your nervous system has learned that your boundaries are negotiable. That you'll make exceptions "just this once" when you're lonely, when you've had wine, when someone is persistent. Every time you hold a boundary—especially when it's hard, especially when you want to make an exception—you are rewriting the code. You're teaching your system: "I mean what I say. My no is a real no. I will not betray you anymore." You defend your Circle of Coherence. No exceptions.

Stay present through the mess without self-judgment. Healing is not linear. As you rebuild coherence, your nervous system will begin to shift from chronic sympathetic activation (fight/flight) into more parasympathetic regulation (rest/repair). But the body holds memory in tissue, in fascia, and in cellular patterns.

You will experience releases—crying, shaking, heat, cold, waves of emotion with no obvious trigger. This is stored activation discharging. Let it move through. You'll feel increased sensitivity as you come out of numbing, feeling more not less. This is not regression. This is your system coming back online. You may feel profound fatigue—healing requires enormous energy, and your body has been in survival mode for decades. Rest is not optional. You'll encounter resistance and sabotage as the old patterns fight to maintain themselves. This is normal. They believe they are keeping you safe.

You will also occasionally slip back into old patterns. What matters is how you respond. Old pattern: shame spiral, self-attack, "I'm broken, I'll never change." New pattern: "I see what happened. I understand why. I recommit to protecting myself. I begin again." Your nervous system needs to see that you will not abandon yourself when you make mistakes. That you'll stay present, stay compassionate, stay committed even when it's messy. The timeline for full healing differs for everyone. Be patient with yourself in a way you never have been before.

My nervous system's strong reaction driving to the farmers market was not evidence of failure. It was evidence that my system is coming back online. That it trusts me enough to communicate clearly—stay away!—because it has seen me respond appropriately to its signals. It has learned that I will do something with that information, even if my action isn't perfect. It sees that we are finally on the same side.

Rebuilding trust isn't about perfection. It is about consistently honoring the signals when they arise. Your nervous system does not need you to never feel fear or agitation. It needs you to respond appropriately and authentically when you do. Not from fear but from respect for your own system's wisdom. Fear says "I can't handle it." Wisdom says "I don't need to handle it—this is not for me." Your nervous system knows the difference.

I've written apologies to my younger self. Had conversations with my higher self. But what seemed to be a missing piece? Thanking my body for sticking with me, for refusing to give up on me and refusing to give out. The best way I can show my gratitude is to listen to it, value it, and give it the care it deserves.

Untamed Truth

You will have moments of fear, grief, and regret. As you stand on the edge of the chrysalis, you'll be tempted to crawl back in. Don't. Feel the feelings, express the emotions, and give your body the rest it needs. Honor what has brought you to this point. Your wings are forming. Your butterfly is calling.
Trust the process.

15

EMERGENCE

········☀········

I stood on the curb in my bathrobe, watching the garbage truck pull up. As it tipped my bin into the compactor, I watched my journals tumble down and disappear. Over 30 years of my life headed to the landfill. Why? Because they weren't me anymore. They were the stories of someone who believed she didn't matter or measure up. They were the relics of a past that no longer defined my future.

The same closet that kept my high school papers also hid a tub full of diaries and journals. One day, as rain poured against the windows, I dragged the tub into the middle of the room and started lining them all up in sequence, starting at age seven. It was a spectacle of kittens, unicorns, flowers, and hearts—images of innocence and imagination. Grabbing a pillow and a cup of mint tea, I settled in, expecting a nostalgic trip down memory lane.

Sporadic and rife with spelling errors, my earliest entries focused on fun—a detailed chronicle of a trip to San Diego and my excitement at getting my first bikini. A few pages and years later, I drew pictures of roller coasters from a trip to Minnesota. The entries got more regular as I prepared to leave the cradle of elementary school and venture into the wild west of sixth grade.

As a daily ritual, I recorded the happenings of my middle school life. There were a lot of things I could have talked about, like the day Barbara Bush and Raisa Gorbachev came to my school or the start of the Gulf War, but there was none of that. Instead, I filled page after page with detailed notes about the boy I liked. Each day I analyzed where I thought I stood with him, like whether he said hi to me in the halls, who he smiled at in class, and whose name was etched on his notebook. If there was no boy news, I would write the date and "nothing," like I ceased to exist without intervention or animation from the boys in my life.

At first, I chuckled and rolled my eyes at how boy-crazy I was and how small my middle school world seemed. It was almost sweet to see how excited I was by a note slipped to me in class or a phone call from a boy I had a crush on. I kept flipping through the pages until a passage caught my eye.

"I would do almost anything to have Jason like me again. My life sucks. I sort of want to commit suicide." I was 11 years old. But then, just days later, I wrote, "I love being in love again."

I started to feel nauseous and dizzy, like I had put on someone else's glasses. I frantically grabbed other diaries, flipping through the pages to find something that felt like me. In my memories, I was the girl with the fire in her belly who, when she got her first tubes of puffy paint, made a sweatshirt that read "BOSS." I was the girl in second grade who kept track of how many boys she could beat in spelling bees and lunchtime arm wrestling. I became the young woman who dropped out of college to travel the country with only a backpack and a dream of freedom. That girl didn't seem to be in there. In her place was a troubled girl turned woman, plagued with anxiety, riddled with self-doubt, and constantly feeling like she was failing.

"Who is this fucking person?!" I yelled as I threw down the diaries in disgust. It felt like a tortured fiction of someone else's life. With my diaries splayed around the room like a crime scene, that anger and judgment morphed into sadness as the memories flooded in. I sobbed bitter tears of regret. "I am so sorry," I wailed. "I am sorry I didn't take better care of us. I am sorry I didn't protect you. I am sorry that I let you believe you were alone and unloved and unworthy. I didn't know."

I didn't know that I would lose myself in an endless search for attention, validation, and security. I didn't know that my desire to feel seen, wanted, and part of something beautiful would lead me to cling to those who reflected back my flawed image of myself, never loving me the way I wanted to be loved. I didn't know that what started as the normal crushes of a boy-crazed pre-teen would keep me searching—for decades—for who or what would make me feel happy and complete. I didn't know how to love *myself*.

That was the pattern: I made others responsible for my happiness and self-worth. When they inevitably couldn't deliver what was never theirs to give, I left, believing they were dragging me down. I left people, jobs, places—thinking everything would be better with something or someone new. But because I hadn't changed what I believed, I would make the same choice again, creating the same kind of situation, ending in me feeling trapped. And so the cycle would repeat.

After the sobs came stillness. I had a choice. I could pack the diaries back up and try to forget about them, or I could make peace with my past and let them go. The untamed truth staring me in the face? That girl wasn't me anymore. There was no value in revisiting the pain, trauma, and anguish of who I no longer was. In tossing the diaries into the trash, I wasn't hiding from my past or shaming the girl who lived it. I was simply embracing who I had become. I was being the butterfly. And butterflies don't carry their cocoons with them—they fly free.

My diaries showed where the static started. But it doesn't really matter when, how, or why it began. The important thing is that I finally saw through the scaffolding of those limiting beliefs to view what was still intact underneath. Under all those beliefs was the shallow pulse of my native signal longing to be revived—the wild heart of autonomy, the rebel yell of courage, the tender touch of compassion. At the center was the pure flame of liberation that could never be extinguished—not by my career, by Max, or by my own kicking of the hive. But reviving my signal wasn't enough. I had to understand the real reason I kept jamming it with static. What was I really afraid of?

The night of my farmers market near miss, as I was lying in bed, it hit me. Hard. If I'm self-sabotaging, I have an excuse for why I don't yet have what I want. The interference served as insurance against existential disappointment. I kept myself small, never letting myself find out what I was truly capable of. I feared I'd never recover from the devastation if I came up short. *What if I give everything and it's not enough? What if I am incapable of doing what I came here to do? What if I am not limitless and free after all?*

Relationships were my most reliable and self-consuming distraction. Because of my wounds growing up and the beliefs they spawned, relationships were where I was willing to abandon myself the most. If I occupied myself with someone who wasn't a true match, who triggered me to perform, caretake, problem-solve, and then grieve, I was too occupied to fully step into my Life Intention, to truly test what life I could live when I'm no longer negotiating against myself. By keeping myself incoherent, I was rebelling against my own fulfillment.

But what I finally realized? The fear of facing my own limit was what was limiting me. That was the cage I built around my dreams. Not any person, circumstance, or situation but my own unwillingness to step up to my own potential. The only thing separating me from what I wanted was me. My passion for liberation, which made any limits or constraints feel unbearable, was my mirror pointing back. Where was I binding myself?

As I sat with that, a wry smile curled my lips. I never needed liberation. Because I was never actually bound by anything but me. My Sovereign Need of Autonomy & Agency wasn't a need to be met—it is who I am. I was always free. What I sought was never in question. It only needed to be believed and embodied. That truth was always there waiting to be untamed. I didn't need to become free, but to live as freedom itself. That is the mastery—seeking fulfillment and finding the truth of you. Then coming into coherence with it in everything you do.

Every Life Intention is a doorway to the same realization. What you sought was never absent, never threatened, never not a part of you. You only believed it was. The seeking itself was the last illusion to release. A Life Intention of harmonization, built on a Sovereign Need of Connection & Belonging, reveals you were never actually separate, never unsupported and alone. A Life Intention of trust, based on Safety & Security, uncovers that you were never actually in danger. The fear was the invitation to your fullest expression, should you be willing to claim it. The practice shifts from yearning and seeking to embodying your untamed truths with unwavering authenticity. When you find your untamed truths within yourself, there is nothing more to find.

Your Blueprint of Being, Life Intention, and Life Design are the path back to who you have always been. Walking this path is your purpose. Your Intention is how you travel it—the specialization that makes it meaningful and exciting to you. The signal you came to master and transmit so that others might see the path too. That is your gift to the world, even if no one ever thanks you, notices, or accepts what you have to offer. It is your contribution to our human collective.

The practice of coming into the Circle of Coherence—"Is it mine?" and "Does it align?"—is the compass leading you home. It is what keeps you on your path. It is the difference between driving on an open highway, having adventures along the way, and circling the roundabout. The roundabout isn't wrong. It isn't a waste or detour—it is showing you where you still need to heal. Every struggle is an invitation to come home.

The proxies, the dream-adjacent distractions, are a pale substitute for the thrill of standing in a life you built entirely through coherent choices and knowing: *I did it. I met myself fully.* That's the fulfillment—knowing that you didn't compromise, didn't hedge, didn't self-sabotage but embodied your pure flame in all its fiery light. You accepted the challenge of your Life Intention and nailed it.

The real fun starts from that point of awareness. What becomes possible when you start believing *everything* is possible? Who can you be when you're not burning up energy performing for worthiness and validation? How good can it get?

Every coherent choice is an opportunity to find out. Every little decision you make in one moment, whether it is to not text him back or to treat yourself to a massage, determines your experience in the next moment. These choices build momentum and strengthen your signal, making you a powerful beacon for what is truly a match and what you will truly enjoy. That is the gift of this work—not just freedom from the static but the power to create a life you love to wake up to each day.

You can start with the next choice that presents itself. Even committing to coherence for just the next seven days or seven weeks will catalyze new potentials. What you'll find is that the static starts to clear, your signal sharpens, and the untamed truths of you step forward to show you the way. Not to a final destination but to continuously expanding joy.

Untamed Truth

We seek what we already are. The path of mastery is a journey home. But we can't find our way until we know who we truly are, what we are here to master, and how we want to live. Coherence is authenticity in action—it is the key that opens the door to a life you love.

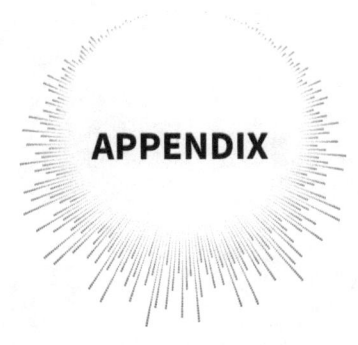

APPENDIX

Supplemental Exercises

16

Supplemental Exercises

Use these exercises if you've completed the main exercises and still aren't certain, or if you want additional confirmation.

Your Blueprint of Being

Your Line in the Sand

This exercise reveals your Sovereign Need and Value through what you can no longer tolerate—the moment when compromise becomes impossible and you finally say "never again."

The Breaking Point

Sometimes we don't discover what matters most by what expands us but by what breaks us. By staying in situations that violate something essential until the cost becomes so unbearable that we finally draw a line in the sand. It's when we know with absolute certainty: *I will never do this to myself again. I am done.*

Think of a time when you compromised yourself in a way that now makes you sick to remember. You stayed in an unhealthy relationship or job far too long. You let someone disrespect you repeatedly. You silenced your truth to keep the peace. You abandoned your own needs to take care of everyone else.

I violated something essential when I tolerated:

What was the cost of that compromise?

Think about your situation and be honest about what you had to ignore, rationalize, or talk yourself out of. What did you have to abandon in yourself to maintain the situation? Where was the inner conflict the loudest?

The highest cost of that compromise was:

What finally made it unbearable?

This is the crucial moment. After all that time tolerating the intolerable, what changed? What was the specific incident, realization, or breaking point that made you know you couldn't do it anymore? What made this time different from all the times before when you tolerated it?

What finally made it unbearable was:

Now complete this sentence with fierce clarity:

"I will never again _____."

This isn't "I'll try not to" or "I should avoid"—this is your line in the sand.

What does this reveal?

The thing you will never again compromise? That's pointing directly to your Sovereign Need. If your declaration is about never again:

- Silencing your truth, overriding your knowing, or giving away your power to choose—you're enabling Autonomy & Agency.

- Abandoning people you love, isolating yourself, or sacrificing relationships—you're enabling Connection & Belonging.

- Letting yourself be diminished, disrespected, or made invisible—you're enabling Dignity & Worth.

- Staying where you can't grow, having your expertise dismissed, or stopping your development—you're enabling Curiosity & Competence.

- Putting yourself in unsafe situations, ignoring red flags, or living in chronic instability—you're enabling Safety & Security.

- Living without purpose, betraying your values, or abandoning what matters most—you're enabling Transcendence & Meaning.

The need you will never again compromise—that's your Sovereign Need. And look at what made your breaking point possible. What quality finally rose up to defend what could no longer be violated? That quality—whether it's courage, integrity, self-respect, honesty, or something else—enabled you to finally honor your Sovereign Need. The value that enables you to stop compromising it is potentially your Sovereign Value.

Your Life Intention

What Keeps Coming Back

Your Life Intention isn't just what you feel or what you're good at—it's what you can't *not* do. It's the theme that shows up across your entire life, the obsession that won't quit, the edge you keep returning to even when you try to walk away. This exercise tracks the external pattern of your Life Intention across time, showing you what's been calling you forward since childhood.

Part A: The childhood obsession

Think back to what you were obsessed with between ages 5-12, before you learned to perform for others. You might think "Barbies!" But what was it that you loved about playing with Barbies? What did you do with your imagination? Keep asking questions until it makes sense. What did you spend hours doing when no one was making you? What kinds of games, activities, or play did you gravitate toward?

What kind of child were you? (Check all that apply)

- The one who had to be in charge / direct the play
- The one who wanted everyone to get along / mediated conflicts
- The one who was always asking "why?" / taking things apart
- The one who needed routine / got upset when plans changed

- The one who stood up to bullies / called out unfairness
- The one who created imaginary worlds / saw magic everywhere

What makes you emotional when you think about that version of you?

Part B: The thing you keep returning to

Look across your entire life—different jobs, relationships, hobbies, roles you've played. What theme keeps showing up, even in wildly different contexts? Examples:

- Always the person organizing / bringing structure to chaos
- Always the bridge-builder / the one connecting divided people or ideas
- Always the calm center / the one others come to for grounding
- Always the truth-teller / the one willing to say what others won't
- Always the dreamer / the one envisioning what could be

My recurring theme is:

Part C: What you can't walk away from

What have you tried to leave behind but can't? Maybe it's a type of work that doesn't pay well, but you keep doing it anyway. Maybe it's a cause you care about even when it's inconvenient. Maybe it's a way of being that others have criticized but you can't stop embodying.

The thing I keep returning to, even when I try to leave it is:

What keeps me coming back to it is:

What it would cost me to walk away from it forever is:

Part D: The convergence

Now look at all three parts together:

- Your childhood obsession (what you loved before you learned to perform)

- Your recurring theme (what shows up across contexts)

- What you can't walk away from (what keeps calling you back)

What's the common thread running through all three?

The theme that's been trying to express itself is:

Your Life Design

Clarifying Through Choice

If your Life Design specifications still feel vague or you're struggling to fill in the blanks, this exercise will help. Sometimes we need to choose between two options to discover what we need.

This isn't about finding the "right" answer—it's about revealing patterns. When forced to choose between appealing options, your gut will show you what your Blueprint requires. Answer quickly.

For each dimension, read each choice pair and circle or mark the option that feels more aligned with who you are. If neither feels right, note what's missing. After completing all choices in a dimension, look for the pattern—what kept showing up?

Your physical environment

Geography & setting
- Neighborhood with neighbors nearby OR Privacy with no one in sight

- Urban density with constant activity OR Rural quiet where you hear silence

- Walking distance to shops, cafes, culture OR Drive required but space and privacy gained

- Proximity to family and old friends OR Distance from history, room for reinvention

Type of space
- Small but perfectly designed for you OR Spacious with room to grow into

- Open flow where spaces connect OR Defined separate rooms with doors

- HOA design rules OR Blank canvas requiring your vision

- Creative space (studio, workshop, music room) OR Multipurpose rooms that adapt

Privacy & community
- Shared resources and favors, borrowing culture OR Complete self-sufficiency

- Space designed to host gatherings OR Intimate scale that protects against invasion

- Shared walls, window visibility OR Buffer zones between you and others

- Strict zoning and design rules OR Full individual autonomy

Circle the themes that appeared most:
Urban density / Rural space / Suburban balance / Remote isolation / Community connection / Private sanctuary / Expansive / Intimate / Self-sufficient / Interdependent / Controlled environment / Wild nature / Hosting capacity / Protected privacy

Your time

Morning rhythm
- Wake naturally without alarms OR Consistent wake time regardless of sleep

- Slow morning routine with space to center OR Rapid mobilization, hit the ground running

- Solo morning before engaging with others OR Morning connection energizes your day

- Same morning structure daily OR Different rhythm depending on day's demands

Peak energy use
- Large uninterrupted blocks for deep work OR Multiple shorter bursts throughout day
- One major focus per day OR Multiple projects in parallel
- Peak hours protected from interruption OR Available but boundaries
- Predictable energy patterns OR Follow intuitive energy as it emerges

Essential boundaries
- Hard stop time, evening is sacred OR Flexible end depending on what's alive
- Communication/meeting blackout periods OR Open schedule but not available on demand
- Clear separation of work and personal time OR Integrated flow between domains
- Scheduled rest and renewal OR Rest when body demands it

Flexibility requirements
- Same weekly template repeating OR Different rhythm each week
- Plan entire week in advance OR Plan day-of based on present state
- Commitments locked once scheduled OR Freedom to

reschedule as energy shifts

- Work within established business hours OR Create your own temporal structure

Circle the themes that appeared most:
Structured routine / Intuitive flow / Protected blocks / Responsive availability / Consistent rhythm / Variable pace / Morning priority / Evening sacred / Deep focus / Collaborative engagement / Hard boundaries / Flexible integration / Scheduled / Spontaneous / Predictable / Adaptive

Your relationships

Types of relationships

- Few deep intimates OR Many varied connections

- Friendships from shared history OR Friendships from shared present interests

- People who match your energy OR People who complement your energy

- Intellectual equals for stimulation OR Emotional equals for vulnerable sharing

Dynamics that must be present

- Mutual respect for autonomy and space OR Daily check-ins and regular contact

- Room for direct honesty without offense OR Kindness and gentleness in all exchanges

- Similar values and worldview OR Different perspectives

that challenge

- Loyalty and long-term commitment OR Presence without claims on the future

Dynamics that cannot be present
- Drama, chaos, or constant crisis OR Boredom, stagnation, or predictability

- Neediness or emotional dependence OR Emotional distance or unavailability

- Critique of your choices OR Passive acceptance without real engagement

- Keeps their word on meeting OR Reschedules as mood and schedule changes

Balance of solitude and connection
- Daily solo time is non-negotiable OR Daily connection is essential

- Solitude to recharge OR Connection to recharge

- Parallel presence (together but separate activities) OR Engaged interaction when together

- Surprise drop-ins are delightful OR Advance notice required for all contact

Circle the themes that appeared most:

Deep intimacy / Broad network / Historical bonds / Present connections / Emotional vulnerability / Intellectual engagement / Direct honesty / Gentle kindness / Growth-oriented / Stable acceptance / Autonomy respected / Regular contact / Long-term loyalty / Present-moment focus / Solitude priority / Connection priority

Your contribution

Primary vehicle
- Direct work with individuals OR Creating resources others use independently

- Creating original work OR Curating and connecting existing ideas

- Visual/artistic expression OR Conceptual/intellectual expression

- Behind-the-scenes influence OR Visible public presence

Essential elements
- Collaboration with others OR Solo execution with full control

- Variety across different domains OR Deep expertise in narrow focus

- Strategic direction and vision OR Tactical implementation and execution

- Defined deliverables and completion OR Ongoing process without clear endpoints

Impact and reach
- Deep transformation for few OR Light touch benefiting many

- Immediate visible impact OR Slow-building legacy over time

- Results you can measure and track OR Ripple effects beyond measurement

- Recognition and visibility for impact OR Anonymous influence without attribution

Creative freedom
- Complete creative control OR Creative direction within structure

- Work that reflects your authentic voice OR Work that translates to broader appeal

- Freedom to experiment and fail OR Reliability and consistent quality

- Define your own standards OR Meet established external standards

Circle the themes that appeared most:
Direct individual impact / Scalable resources / Written expression / Spoken expression / Building systems / Catalyzing change / Original creation / Curation & connection / Visual/artistic / Conceptual/intellectual / Public presence / Behind-scenes influence / Collaboration / Solo control / Deep expertise / Broad vari-

ety / Immediate impact / Legacy building / Local tangible / Global reach / Creative freedom / Strategic structure

Final integration

You've now forced choices across all four dimensions. The patterns that emerged aren't random—they're your Blueprint speaking through preference and instinct. Your specifications should now feel less like aspirational wishes and more like concrete requirements—the actual conditions under which your Blueprint flourishes.

17

COHERENCE AUDIT: WEEKLY REALITY CHECK

Use this weekly to detect where interference is operating. Answer quickly—first thought, gut response. You're looking for friction, not analysis. Tell yourself the truth about anywhere you are frustrated, annoyed, or fearful.

Material/Physical Domain - *Resources, environment, body*

- What in my physical environment drains my energy?
- What am I tolerating about my living situation?
- Where do I feel financial stress or restriction?
- What is my body trying to tell me that I'm ignoring?

Relational Domain - *Partnership, family, friendship, community*

- Which relationships leave me depleted?
- Where am I performing instead of being myself?
- What conversation am I avoiding?

- Where do I feel resentment building?

Creative Domain - *Work, service, contribution, expression*

- What about my work creates dread?
- Where do I feel like I'm going through the motions?
- What am I doing out of obligation rather than alignment?
- What would I do if external validation didn't matter?

Mental/Emotional Domain - *Beliefs, patterns, self-talk*

- What thoughts keep looping without resolution?
- What am I trying to convince myself of?
- What emotion am I suppressing to keep the peace?
- What fear is making my decisions?

Spiritual/Energetic Domain - *Practices, connection, intuition*

- What is my intuition saying that I'm overriding?
- Where am I using spiritual concepts to avoid hard truths?
- What synchronicity or pattern am I dismissing?
- What do I know that I'm pretending not to know?

Sovereignty Domain - *Boundaries, autonomy, self-trust*

- What boundary am I not holding?
- Where am I seeking permission for what's mine to decide?
- What micro-betrayal did I commit against myself this week?
- Where did I override my knowing to keep someone else comfortable?

Time/Energy Domain - *How you spend your time and energy*

- What am I saying yes to that should be no?
- What tasks exhaust me?
- What matters most that I'm not making time for?
- Where does my calendar reflect someone else's priorities?

Pattern Recognition: Look across all domains. What theme emerges? Where is the interference loudest? That's your coherence work for the week.

Acknowledgements

This book benefited from the thoughtful feedback of several early readers willing to roll up their sleeves and help me finetune my framework. Thank you to Amber Dykes, whose logic, rigor, and willingness to go deep provided critical improvements to the Part I chapters. Your "goosebump tests" are gold! I would also like to thank Christy Phillips, Julia Thie, Rachel Blasioli, and Maria Martins for giving me their time, thoughts, and reactions as I refined the exercises. I am grateful for the publishing advice, tips, and ongoing friendship and support of fellow author and long-time bestie, Deirdre Hall. I'd also like to thank my parents for rolling with the punches, raising me to be resourceful and self-sufficient, and supporting me even when they disagreed with my decisions. And to Ezzy and Tish, thank you for the cuddles and comic relief during long days of writing and editing.

I want to acknowledge Kelly Thebo and the Collective—your teaching and mentoring became my remembering. I am forever grateful for your candor, insistence that I tell myself the truth, and encouragement as I got my wings and learned to fly free. I also want to acknowledge the early coaching and support of Nea Clare, whose visioning exercise dared me to dream of the life I now live. Acknowledgments are also due to the Academy for Coaching Excellence, whose foundational courses planted seeds for what became the Untamed Truths framework. I would also like to acknowledge everyone whose story became a teachable moment for this book. Together is how we grow.

Finally, thank you, dear readers, for being part of a dream come true. I am grateful and humbled to be part of your journey to unwavering authenticity. May you live your untamed truths!

About the Author

Carolyn Brouillard has spent three decades exploring consciousness and the art of authentic living. She is a corporate dropout turned author and teacher. Her expertise is forged at the intersection of extremes—from riding freight trains as a teenage punk to climbing the corporate ladder to reclaiming self-sovereignty. Her work bridges spiritual insight and real-world application, delivering actionable frameworks for personal transformation. As the founder of Untamed Press, she is dedicated to supporting bold voices whose lived wisdom, courage, and authentic presence offer revelatory perspectives that transform the human experience.

When Carolyn isn't writing or teaching, she loves to hike, kayak, stargaze, and explore new places. She lives in the Blue Ridge Mountains, where the wild spirit of the forests, lakes, and rivers serves as her constant inspiration.

Join the journey at www.youruntamedtruths.com, where you can access free resources and sign up for coaching programs, workshops, and events.

Thank you for reading *Your Untamed Truths*.
If you enjoyed it, please consider leaving an online review, such as on Amazon or Goodreads, and recommending it to your circle. Word-of-mouth helps independent authors reach the people who could benefit from their work.

Want to share this book? Join the affiliate program at www.bookshop.org to earn commission on book sales while supporting independent bookstores. Already earning as an Amazon Associate? Please consider promoting this book.

To download the printable companion workbook for this book and explore additional resources and upcoming events, visit: www.youruntamedtruths.com and sign up for the newsletter.

To learn about Untamed Press, visit: www.untamedpress.com.

UNTAMED
PRESS

www.ingramcontent.com/pod-product-compliance
Lightning Source LLC
LaVergne TN
LVHW091539070526
838199LV00002B/130